10 X

IMAGINATION
AS SPACE OF FREEDOM

IMAGINATION

AS SPACE
OF
FREEDOM

DIALOGUE BETWEEN THE EGO AND THE UNCONSCIOUS

by Verena Kast

Translated from the German by Anselm Hollo

**Fromm International
Publishing Corproation
New York**

Grateful acknowledgment is made to Pro Helvetia, the Swiss Council for the Arts, for subsidizing the translation of this work.

Translation Copyright © 1993
Fromm International Publishing Corporation, New York

Originally published in 1988 as *Imagination als Raum der Freiheit*
Copyright © 1988, Walter-Verlag AG, Olten

Printed in the United States of America

First U.S. Edition

Library of Congress Cataloging-in-Publication Data

Kast, Verena, 1943-
[Imagination als Raum der Freiheit. English]
Imagination as space of freedom : dialogue between the ego and the unconscious / Verena Kast ; translated from the German by Anselm Hollo. -- 1st U.S. ed.
p. cm.
Translation of : Imagination als Raum der Freiheit.
Includes bibliographical references.
ISBN 0-88064-202-5 : $19.95
1. Imagination -- Therapeutic use. I. Title.
RC489.F35K3713   1993   92-28251
616.89'14--dc20   CIP

*To my grandfather, who introduced me
to the world of imagination*

CONTENTS

In the land of fairy tales
poetry blooms
I look for it
on the dreampath
that guides me

Rose Ausländer

Introductory Remarks

THE LITERATURE concerning imaginative procedures is extensive. Why write yet another book about them?

A pivotal influence on the use of imagination in therapy and in the individuation process emanates from C.G. Jung and his technique of Active Imagination. This technique, however, is hardly mentioned anymore in those numerous publications; Active Imagination, one of the most fundamental methods of imagining, is known only to a few specialists. Even these don't always appreciate it because it is considered difficult.

To me, it seems essential to enable therapy clients to gain access to the space of imagination, and I believe that Active Imagination is an outstanding means to this end. Admittedly, many people have to practice it at first, while others may master it without further instruction.

This book addresses itself to those learning the technique of imagining as well as those who wish to gain even greater access to the space of imagination, and to therapists who use imagining in their work. Imaginative abilities are natural abilities, and when put to use and practiced, they can open up a new Lebensraum.

The present book evolved out of my practical work with clients designed to introduce them to imagining, and to gradually lead them to Active Imagination. Hence I frequently provide the possible instructions for imagining which I use in my practice. These instructions should be taken as suggestions. They are intended to guide the reader inspired by this book to exercise his or her own imaginative faculties.

Diverse possibilities in the realm of imagination and particular problems arising in this context are illustrated by means of exemplary cases. These examples, too, may serve to familiarize one with the space of imagination.

My heartfelt thanks to all who have given me permission to use their imaginings or parts of them in this book.

Particular thanks are due to Mrs. Christa Henzler, certified social education worker, for her active participation in thinking through the final version of the manuscript, and for the great care she has taken with it.

Verena Kast
St. Gallen, September 1987

Imagination as Space of Freedom

THE SPACE OF IMAGINATION is the space of freedom—a space in which, in an entirely natural manner, boundaries are crossed, space and time relativized, and possibilities we no longer or do not yet have are made available to experience. While the space of imagination is the space of memory, it is also, and primarily, the space of the future brought into the present and made relevant. In the imagination, much becomes possible that we don't consider to be so, much that we even regard as sheer fantasy. In our imaginings, we see a reflected image of our psyche with its wishes, fears, longings, and creative possibilities. Situations we have already experienced can be re-experienced one more time. Thanks to our imaginative abilities we can put ourselves into another person's position and relate to his or her feelings. With our imagination we are able to conceive of change, of how a given situation could be altered.

Furthermore, even experienced reality becomes a symbol in our imagination: becomes, as it were, a middle ground between concretely experienced reality and our connection to our psychic background. The imagination exists in a relationship with the exterior, apperceptible concrete world, creates an image of it, changes our way of experiencing it, and thus in turn transforms the exterior, apperceptible world. Although the imagination has much to do with our "interior world," as long as it remains productive it never loses touch with the exterior; on the other hand, it does not subordinate itself to that exterior world but always transcends it.

The Concept of Imagination

CHAPTER ONE

WHEN WE SPEAK OF IMAGINING, we refer to the activity of our imaginative power, our capacity for fancy, our fantasies, our daydreams.

Even though these phenomena may differ from one another, they all exist in the imaginative realm, and as long as no particular distinctions clamor to be made, I will start out by using simply the term "imagination."[1] Our human imaginative abilities enable us to have a more or less vivid picture of something that is no longer or not yet there—or that may never "be there" at all. These imaginings can be very pictorial, characterized by colors or shapes, but they can also express themselves by means of olfactory memory or anticipation, tactile memory or fantasy, or acoustic memories or expectations. They can also be a of a more intellectual nature.

Our power of imagination manifests itself most impressively in our creations in the fine arts, painting, literature, music, but also in the development of scientific hypotheses. It is also a prerequisite for all intellectual flights of fancy, regardless of whether or not they can be realized, and whether they solve or create more problems.

We owe our creative works to that power, and these works, in turn, stimulate it. Consider literature: it appears specifically designed to stimulate the imagination and to enable us to empathize imaginatively with the diverse characters it presents.

Despite this great significance for human culture and life in general, the imaginative faculty does not enjoy an exclusively positive reputation. We don't doubt that we have to thank it for magnificent works, but we can also be frightened by it. This is evident in the expression, we "just imagined" something—which means that something exists only in the imagination, that we have merely deluded ourselves into thinking it was real, that someone no longer sees reality correctly and has replaced it with fantasy.

Our imaginings can help us comprehend the world and reveal what will happen in certain situations. They can help us empathize and emotionally comprehend a situation more or less correctly, but they can also distort our perception of reality, especially when they are predominantly determined by our problems. Thus, a very vivid imaginative notion of how people "should be" may distort our view of a real person in a relationship so that his or her actions are interpreted according to our imaginings.[2] The very word "imagination" has overtones of fantasy and illusion and contains the possible meaning of something being "merely" imaginary, not corresponding to any reality. Here, a sense of fear becomes evident, the fear that a person might emigrate to the realm of the imaginary, leave the common world of what is regarded as real for an "unreal world," and hence be lost to the "real world," the one people share. The expression "power of imagination" demonstrates that it is a force we are dealing with, a dynamic we have to take into account, capable of changing us and worthy of our apprehension.

The word "imagination" evokes two kinds of expectation: we know that no creative solutions, no matter how mundane, can be reached without it. Everybody has to rely on his or her imagination in dealing with the everyday, yet the solutions can't be too fantastic, too unrealistic. The imagination, the space of freedom, the condition of creative transformations—creations—is also a space of fear: there is the danger that this space alienates us from "reality," draws us away from the everyday world. That, however, is its task: the world of imagination is a world of other possibilities open to us. It expresses human longing for the "utterly other"—for, finally, the divine, and for our own chances to experience the "utterly other" and even to shape it while entering into a dialogue with it.

The longing for the "utterly other" may grow so powerful that it disrupts the balance of the stimulating dialogue between the everyday world and the world of the imagination.

Perception and Imagination

CHAPTER TWO

THE WORLD OF THE IMAGINATION is fascinating and frightening. While it can add new dimensions to everyday life, it is also a world in which it is possible to get lost—in everyday speech, this is referred to as "losing touch with reality" or "becoming unrealistic." There are times when those terms are also applied to people in the process of developing creative ideas before those developments are properly understood.

Such designations show our tendency to regard the exterior, concretely perceivable world—which we assume to be perceived by all people in a roughly similar way, although this is not true in such absolute terms—as real, and the interior world as unreal. Hence we are invited, now and again, to perform a reality check, to ask ourselves whether what we imagine truly coincides with reality, with the concrete world. It may indeed be useful to compare one's own perception of a situation, to which many personal notions contribute, with another person's view; but the perceptions of any one person are never totally "real," nor are those of another totally "unreal"—two realities are juxtaposed and may influence each other.

To regard reality that depends essentially on our perception of the exterior, concrete world as *the* reality, and to describe the reality that is based mostly on our imaginative conceptions as non-reality, is a questionable proposition.

When a child afraid of dogs meets an actual dog, its fantasy image of a dog—"a big hound that attacks me, knocks me over, puts its paw on my chest, its mouth open with many large and terrifying teeth, its tongue hanging out"—strikes it as much more real and impressive than any comment to the effect that the dog in this case is a dear old, slightly lame, toothless canine and nothing to be afraid of, even if that comment is a far more accurate description of reality than the child's fantasy image. But the attempt to direct the child's attention to the fact that this particular dog does not fit his interior fright image of the animal may give him the idea that there are, possibly, different kinds of dogs, and that he ought to take a look and evaluate the degree of danger.

Dealing and working with imaginative conceptions is apt to make one realize one thing: we can't start out from the position that one person is fully aware of the reality of his or her situation, while another person is not. It makes a great deal of sense to communicate to each other exactly how we perceive a given situation, to begin a possibly productive dialogue instead of arguing about who is "right"—which is not very stimulating and usually does not solve problems.

The suspicion towards imaginative thought, rather clearly articulated in the fear that a person may use his or her imaginative faculties to drift too far from commonly perceived and shared reality, also emphasizes that the dialogue between perception and imagination has to be kept alive.

Perception and imagination are connected in a particular way: we perceive external stimuli, but if we turn these off, for example, by closing our eyes—we are able to imagine what we just perceived. Yet we also know that we subject the perception to slight alterations: thus, a region that we once explored looks somewhat different in our imagination, and when we return to it, we may be surprised how much larger the vistas are than those we remembered. We then use this new perception to correct our memory's image of it.

On the other hand, we complement our perceptions with conceived notions. If we are not able to perceive something clearly because it appears too nebulous or because we have too little to go on, we fill in the gaps with our imagination until we get an unambiguous impression. A great deal of research in gestalt psychology relates to this circumstance.[3] We also know games in which one person starts drawing a picture and we are asked to guess what it represents. Often it takes only a few lines to indicate what the object is—yet sometimes we guess wrong, in the direction of our interior expectations.

The less information we have with which to create an image, the more we rely on our conceptual ability and power of imagination to compose an "unambiguous picture" of a situation. We need this in order to deal with anxiety, to achieve an interior equilibrium which allows us to get our bearings and an overview. When we are in a psychic state that restricts our ability to receive information, as in the state of total rage, our imagining or visualization of a situation replaces our actual perception of it.

We have to assume that perception and imagination share pathways in the brain. The question has been researched in various ways.[4] Particularly well known, simple, and convincing are the researches of Segal[5] who in 1971 studied the so-called Perky phenomenon. In 1910, Perky discovered that people who are asked to imagine a specific object on an empty canvas are no longer able to recognize an actual, faint projection of that object on the canvas. On the other hand, subjects who have not tried to imagine an object on the blank canvas are quite able to see that projection. Segal conducted further research on the phenomenon and found it to be a universal human experience. This, however, means that it is possible to block external stimuli by imaginative means. It is to be noted that this is true only when the external signal belongs to the same modality as the imagined one: visual stimuli are not perceived if the imagined object is also visual. Auditory stimuli, on the other hand, can be perceived while the imagination is engaged in the visual sphere.

This recognition indicates that our imagination is one channel for our processing of everyday information. The research also indicates the usefulness of blocking external stimuli, e.g. by closing our eyes or staring at a fixed point, when we wish to follow a stream of interior images.

It may well be that it is our power to imagine which creates a meaningful whole out of the discrete bits of information perceived and received by the brain. Kant pointed this out long ago. He regarded the imagination as "a necessary ingredient of perception itself": "imagination has to bring the manifold of intuition into the form of an image."[6]

Eccles, the well-known cerebro-neurophysiologist, furthermore points out the familiar fact that "conscious perception derived from some general sensory input becomes largely modified by emotions, feelings, and desires."[7] This means that even when, on the level of sensation, we all hold the roughly same images in mind, these are instantly linked to additional, related bits of information from our life stories and assigned appropriate emotional responses. Thus we always have a very individual "view" of things.

In psychoanalytical terms this means that our complexes determine our ability to comprehend information as well as our ability to evaluate it.[8] As Eccles emphasizes, this is indeed a phenomenon with which we are all familiar. We notice that a fearful person sees causes for fear everywhere or experiences the frightening aspect of a situation with particular intensity. When, for instance, a child on a swing screams out of enjoyment and excitement combined with fear, such a person only perceives that the child might fall down and is therefore frightened, but does not realize the child's enjoyment of his own courage. Such projections always reveal something about one's emotional attitude at the moment. When compared over a longer period of time, they also provide information about our major emotional problems and possibilities.

If we manage to change our imaginative projections, we also become able to influence the emotions related to them and to change our moods.

In sum, it can be said that the imagination is a fundamental organizing principle in our processing of information and emotions. The power of imagination either accompanies our more or less conscious perceptions in the form of a ceaseless flow of images, or, in the extreme opposite case, as consciously shaped fantasy. It is the prerequisite for all creative work but also the prerequisite for mystical experience. The ability to imagine things inheres in every human being and is employed, consciously or unconsciously, both in the solution of everyday problems and in the creation of a world that momentarily seems more satisfying than the one we inhabit.

Eccles considers our power to imagine equal to our intelligence as an entirely essential capability of our brain. In his opinion, we can't learn how to imagine, since the ability to do so is a given, nor can we lose that ability, not even in advanced age.[9] Even though we don't have to acquire imaginative ability by learning, I believe we can improve it by practice and use it much more consciously than we customarily do.

The capacity to change preconceived notions is extraordinarily important in the management of everyday problems: just consider how frequently we project imagined scenarios of important situations and second-guess our own behavior and the behavior of other participants.

But the realm of conception, of imagination, extends much further. Bachelard, for instance, mocks psychologists who use or misuse the imagination "only" for experiments;[10] in his view, imagined things make up a separate world, a world of poetry. In his opinion, the human being is—among other things—a creature of the imagination, and imagination does not necessarily make us more efficient in our daily actions, but it does enhance our poetic side. I consider this a very important way of looking at the question. It points out that the imagination is where we encounter such an entirely "other" side of ourselves. Nevertheless, it is so easy to experience in everyday life—and is, finally, just a part of everyday life.

Speaking of the creative imagination, Corbin says that it mediates between the visible and the invisible, between the physical and the spiritual world. Hence it is the medium that enables one to love in a person the divine being that expresses itself.[11]

Speaking about Active Imagination—the method C. G. Jung proposed for psychotherapy, which involves vivification of interior images and giving voice to interior figures to activate a deep stratum of the psyche while then dealing with these images and voices with a wide-awake ego—Jung calls it a method in which the imagining person not only analyzes his or her unconscious but also gives it a chance to analyze the ego complex.[12] This dialogue between the ego and the unconscious is the prerequisite for the individuation process, the psychic process in the course of which a person becomes what he or she ultimately is.

The imagination is an entirely human phenomenon and has always been used and described as such: Socrates conversed with his daimon, and the mystics have left us texts which we would, today, classify as imaginings, texts in which they tell us about seeing God or looking into their own souls and examining them.

Imagining as Therapy

CHAPTER THREE

ALL SCHOOLS OF THERAPY use the imagination, in an either more or less conscious way. Every form of therapy that deals with memory and expectation, with fears and hopes, finds itself compelled to work with a person's imaginative abilities.

This holds true in therapies in which the experience and understanding of dreams is regarded as important as well as in behavioral therapies grounded in the belief that the power of imagination contains possibilities for change. For a comprehensive overview of the various imaginative methods, see Singer's *Imagery and Daydream: Methods in Psychotherapy and Behavior Modification.*[13]

A fundamental distinction can be made between forms of therapy that work almost exclusively with imaginings, e.g., Desoille and Leuner 's,[14] and others that use imaginative procedures. It is my intention to examine the therapeutic possibilities of imaginings, and to demonstrate how imaginings can be used in therapy and imaginative abilities can be developed. Finally, I want to describe a path from imagining to Active Imagination.

When we work with imaginings in a therapeutic context, we express the belief that it is possible for us to use them to work on our images of ourselves and the world, and to become conscious of the fact that these images of ourselves and of the world may be either helpful or detrimental to our ability to manage our lives.

We also show that we consider it essential to deal with emotions, which are of course also expressed in the images that occur, i.e., we show that it is essential to truly experience emotions because this both frees energies for action and enables one to experience one's relationship with oneself. Psychotherapeutic work with and out of images has its antecedents in work with dream images in Freud, Jung, and others. Dealing with our dream images and, indeed, all other images, we come to see not only that they tell us something about ourselves but that they can also bring about changes in our experience of ourselves and the world. Diagnostic and therapeutic aspects may be recognized in these dream images, and such diagnostic and therapeutic aspects inhere in all interior imagery.

Every image we describe, draw, create tells us something about ourselves, tells us something about where we find ourselves in each instance. This is so because we only have certain images at our disposal in any given situation, be they images of memory or anticipation. They say something about our current condition. In this sense, every diagnosis based on images is a process diagnosis. It reveals where a person stands at a given moment in the process of his or her development, what problems have to be engaged, what vital possibilities for the future are depicted in those images, which longings indicate a line of development. When one deals with people over a longer period of time it becomes apparent that some images are not quite so closely related to specific situations as they may seem at first, but that certain types of images recur. The easiest way to realize this is by looking at ourselves: among the multitude of images we are able to create in dreams, fantasies, etc., we discover multiple variations of a few basic images.

Our images always reflect our momentary view of ourselves and the world, our view of present relational possibilities. Such self-comprehension is always therapeutically valuable.

Therapeutic effects brought about by the use of imaginings (in a stricter sense) become evident when the analysand finds that work on the images opens up additional perspectives of experience and action to him or her. "Fixed notions" are replaced by diverse possibilities of experience—and thus action—by means of a process in which concentration on particular images causes these to change either spontaneously, or through a therapist's intervention in the imaginative process.

In this process, a closeness to emotions is gained, and when we can truly feel an emotion, this generates energies for action. On the other hand, distance may be gained from extremely negative notions about ourselves, and images of longing may reveal essential personality aspects that have not been sufficiently integrated into everyday life.

One's sense of oneself changes; it is possible to realize that life, in the sense of personality change, can be shaped creatively.

It goes without saying that such an engagement with imaginative faculties may also result in an intrinsically creative, possibly even poetic stance toward life. It is very common to encounter the emotion of hope in our imaginings, since they are frequently directed toward the future and the transcendence of boundaries of time and space. Even where the medium of imagination largely reflects our wishes, it brings us closer to the feeling that situations may change, that the future is still open.

To hope is not simply to build castles in the air: it is, finally, a confidence in life's ability to support us, a confidence that all of life and one's own intentions can be brought into a shared context, even in the future. In the emotion of hope we experience a fundamental security. [15] But it is precisely this therapeutically effective experience of hope that is denied to us when the images are kept far from our emotions, hence far from ourselves, and in that sense are most similar to what we call "castles in the air."

It is the task of therapeutic work with the imaginative faculty to bring these images closer to the ego. The more intense our involvement with our images becomes, the greater their significance to us will be, and the more likely it is that we may be able to have experiences comparable to those the mystics had.

Since imaginings have an inherent tendency to cross boundaries, expand them, create new ones, there is also a tendency to regard their efficaciousness and their sphere of influence as "boundless." We need to recognize certain limitations: there are people who find it easy to get in touch with their unconscious by means of images created by their imaginative faculties, and others for whom the methods of drawing or psychodrama are more appropriate. These methods become most effective when we succeed in concentrating intensely on the interior images, i.e., when we manage to scrutinize them closely, get right next to them.

The converse also holds true: when we succeed in seeing the interior images precisely, in immersing ourselves in them, we eventually gain greater powers of concentration in our everyday lives.

The Method of Imagining

CHAPTER FOUR

Concentrating on Images

One concentrates one's attention on some impressive but unintelligible dream-image, or on a spontaneous visual impression, and observes the changes taking place in it. Meanwhile, of course, all criticism must be suspended and the happenings observed and noted with absolute objectivity. . . . Under these conditions, long and often very dramatic series of fantasies ensue. The advantage of this method is that it brings a mass of unconscious material to light. Drawing, painting, and modelling can be used to the same end. Once a visual series has become dramatic, it can easily pass over into the auditive or linguistic sphere and give rise to dialogues and the like.[16]

WHAT JUNG ESSENTIALLY DESCRIBES HERE, as a particular "stated method of introspection," is not yet quite his method of Active Imagination, but the imagining that may become Active Imagination once the dialogue of our consciousness with the unconscious has been set in motion.

Nevertheless, this methodical prescription applies to all kinds of imagining: imagining begins with an image that preoccupies us.

By starting out with concentration on such an image—

and simultaneously shutting off perceptions of the exterior world—it becomes possible to perceive the changes in these interior images and their flow. We achieve this state of interior attention best when we're able to disconnect our critical faculties, or when we include them merely as something that also belongs to us and that need not disrupt the observation of the interior image flow. An attitude of curiosity which simply absorbs and assumes things is the least disruptive to our image sequence. Criticism can be postponed.

The interior image flow must not only be perceived but also preserved in some form. Interior images are very fleeting and easily escape from consciousness. One way of shaping them consists of the attempt to verbalize or to draw the sequence of events.

Furthermore, Jung points out that the images have to be observed with "absolute objectivity." It can hardly be assumed that Jung, who knows so much about the influences emanating from the unconscious that prevent us from being "objective," truly believes in "absolute objectivity." It seems to me he merely wants to emphasize that these sequences of fantasies, the flow of images, should be perceived as such, if possible without critical distortions caused by our consciousness—but also that we should first of all see and accept these fantasies as "the other" in ourselves.

By recording the images, we become able to deal with them. Even when certain images keep besetting us, we are able to detach ourselves from them without suppressing them.

And that is the extent of Jung's methodical advice. In this context, Jung does not mention relaxation, a method used today in most imaginative procedures.

Relaxation

Generally speaking, relaxation enhances the intensity of affective reactions. In a relaxed state, imaginings become more vivid, more emotional, more relevant to the imaginer. They are, in other words, experienced by the ego with greater closeness and resonance and deserve greater commitment, since they are more capable of changing our mood.[17] The experience of interior images, in turn, enhances relaxation. This causes the images to become even more vivid, and a feedback loop is created.[18] When imaginings are created in a therapeutic context, a certain degree of relaxation is achieved by the imaginer's sense of being in a familiar analytical situation and secure within its solid framework. I believe, nevertheless, that further methods of relaxation may be helpful in this regard.

Images may be created in a sitting or reclining position. The sitting position seems preferable since it still indicates a posture, a containment, and this will prove important for Active Imagination.

Imaginative techniques require twofold attention. On one hand, the psyche has to let things happen, has to let the images flow; on the other, these images have to be perceived and either formulated immediately or retold later. They have to be retained in some form. It isn't merely a matter of passive surrender to our image world, letting oneself be carried away by it, but it is also a question of grasping this world and structuring it. It seems to me that the sitting position is particularly suited to the achievement of this dual attitude toward the images.

Eyes are closed, or the gaze is fixed on a point, to make it possible to concentrate on our interior imaginings. In most cases, I begin the relaxation exercises by asking the imaginer to rest her or his feet on the ground and to be aware of both ground and feet. This results in an additional containment, a grounding in the body. Next, I advise the client to relax his or her shoulders and to breathe out in a deep sigh. The sigh enables people to be aware of their center without being specifically asked to do so, and it also begins the first stage of relaxation.

I keep reminding the client that tension can be released continuously by breathing out. If necessary, I remind him or her to become aware of different parts of the body and to free them from tension by breathing out and conducting the tension into the ground via legs and feet. When the entire body has been attended to and relaxed as far as possible, I ask the client to perceive the body as a whole and to release any tensions that are still felt—or else to accept them as parts of him or her in this situation. Then I ask her or him to focus on seeing the interior flow of images.

There are many ways to achieve relaxation.[19] A simple form of relaxation consists of asking the client to tense one part of the body after another as strongly as possible and then to let go. People familiar with autogenic training will find it easy to relax by having it suggested to them that individual parts of the body become "warm and heavy."

The relaxation employed has to be agreeable to the therapist and suited to the client. To my mind, the question of the duration of the relaxed state is more important than the method used to achieve it.

Cautela and McCullough,[20] both behavioral therapists, relate that they use about fifteen minutes to tense and relax the main muscle groups before proceeding to concentration on an interior image. They also suggest that clients practice relaxation at home. Leuner[21] writes that the therapist should give the patient "a brief request to relax."

There are widely divergent ideas about how thoroughly relaxed people should be in order to reach their images, but this also depends on the individual client. The purpose of relaxation is to diminish the state of over-wakefulness, so that a right-hemisphere perception becomes more possible and integral image-thinking is stimulated. It is also possible that relaxation gives us a sense of being secure in our bodies and thus enables us to experience images of security for the first time. This makes it easier to start dealing with the interior images.

When I engage in imaginative work with individuals, I try to determine the duration of relaxation by my own intuitive sense of the situation. The duration may be modified later if it becomes apparent that a shorter or longer period of relaxation would be more pleasurable.

In a group situation, I extend relaxation exercises to the point where I believe I can clearly observe a state of relaxation. The question of the depth of relaxation also depends on the length of time available: a good state of relaxation leads to more vivid, more colorful, longer, more emotional imaginative processes.

On Dealing with Images

Some people talk while engaging in the imagining process, and this works particularly well when the therapist participates in it and assists it when necessary.

In non-therapeutic situations, a tape recorder may be used, as long as it is not felt to be distracting.

Others relate what they have seen and experienced at the end of the process. They mostly "get stuck" in places where an intervention by the therapist would have been useful. After a brief period of relaxation and a discussion about how to proceed in the particular situation, the image can be replayed—and changed. Since the interior flow of images is experienced in visual terms, many people find it difficult to represent the images verbally, for that is a left-hemisphere activity;[22] they prefer to represent their images by drawing them.

It is extremely important to record the images in some form, but it is difficult to record them adequately. To me, it seems particularly important not to translate the visual impression too hastily into language. For the sake of an integral comprehension of this image world, it is necessary to be able to see the images as well as to describe them—in other words, to perceive them in terms of both hemispheres. If we leave an image too quickly, we run the danger of neglecting the emotion linked to it and thus preventing an experience of the self and a possible change of attitude.

It also seems particularly important to me, especially in regard to Active Imagination, in which dialogue plays a part, not to lose the quality of the image as an image but to retain it to its full extent.

In a group, I proceed by having each member tell the image sequences and then draw them, write them down, or act them out as a psychodrama. Groups should be kept small (six to eight persons).[23]

Indication and Contra-Indication

Since the imagination is a fundamental human faculty for the processing of information and thus also a means of orientation, and since it also provides a possibility to experience emotions and to deal with them, it impresses me as a technique that should be considered in every therapeutic effort designed to render people more genuine and autonomous, to bring them into a closer relationship with their unconscious and their fellow humans, and finally to teach them how to deal more creatively and empathetically with themselves and the world.

The technique seems particularly indicated when people have to be brought closer to their emotions, when there is a need to see present life problems from a more symbolic point of view, and also when feelings of emptiness and negative feelings are prevalent and create more negative thoughts, which in turn render those feelings even more negative.

Imaginative procedures also seem useful in the processing of dreams and actual emotionally stressful situations, likewise in the integration of fractured complexes.

The technique seems contra-indicated in the case of people who, even after prolonged training, are unable to see images or always experience these diffusely—whose imagination, in other words, does not animate them. It also seems contra-indicated for people who are able to produce flowery strings of fantasies with a certain facility but are not emotionally moved by them. It may, of course, be possible to use therapeutic interventions to create greater emotional closeness to their images. If this proves impossible, not much change can be expected from this technique.

It is contra-indicated in acute or chronic psychoses or in the case of pronounced obsessive symptoms. Leuner[24] does not deem the procedure suitable for pronounced depressive states, but this is contradicted by research results of this therapy on depressive patients who had been psychiatrically hospitalized, as described by Schultz.[25]

In the long run, the dangers of imaginative procedures seem to have been overestimated.[26] There has been a fear of reactive psychotic episodes, but these occur only rarely. An excessive flood of images may mostly be stopped by means of a change in body posture, stimulation of perceptions of the exterior world, and exact description and recording of the images.

The imaginative faculty is a natural one, available to one and all, and coupled with our intelligence, offers outstanding potential for human spirituality. Eccles[27] emphasizes this over and over again. We can use it and develop it. When it threatens to become dangerous, we react with defense mechanisms and immediately turn our primary attention to other realms of life. Work with the imagination is by no means restricted to therapy; imaginative people have always engaged in it. In therapy, however, the work with imaginative faculties is conducted in a very goal-oriented manner.

It is, of course, always possible to escape into fantasy, just as it is possible to escape into intelligence, rationality, etc. The perennial fear that people engaged in imagining become less and less able to distinguish the imagined from the real has not proved justified; rather the opposite seems to be the case. Concentrating on imaginative aspects, people become more aware as they complement their perception of the world with imagined notions.

Guided Imagining

CHAPTER FIVE

INITIALLY, guided imaginings, i.e., processes in which the therapist presents suggestions, may serve to train a person's imaginative abilities and to make it evident that these interior images really exist and are not all that difficult to perceive. In these guided imaginings, imaginers don't have to concentrate on looking for spontaneous changes that may arise in their images: these changes are suggested to them from outside. However, the imaginers are told that they don't have to follow these suggestions if their images do change spontaneously.

In group practice, starting points for imaginings may be dream motifs, or, should no suitable oneiric images present themselves, symbols may be used that are both vivid and have many layers of meaning.

Example: The House Motif

After a brief period of relaxation, the following directions are given:

Imagine the house (a house) of your childhood. Walk around the house, take a good look at it. Enter one of its rooms. What does it look like? Can you sense a certain smell? Do you meet

someone there, or do you see an object that attracts your atten-
tion? Leave that room again. Look at the house again and think
about rebuilding it. Rebuild it. Now detach yourself from the
images of this house and imagine a house in which you would be
pleased to live. And now imagine a fantastic house, one that
does not exist yet, a utopian house—not necessarily one to be
lived in . . . Now detach yourself from your images, open your
eyes, stretch, yawn . . . Then let the interior images pass by your
eyes one more time.

It is advisable to have imaginers detach themselves from
their images in a very conscious manner, particularly by
encouraging body movements, since these will stop the
interior images—even if they prove quite distressing—
from dominating the imaginers' consciousness.[28]

This guided imagining on the house motif convinces the
imaginer that everybody is indeed able to create an image
of something even in the absence of exterior stimuli. The
various images will, of course, be of varying degrees of
vividness. The example I have chosen demonstrates the
diverse possibilities of the imagining. In the case of imagining a childhood house, it is an exercise of memory. The
instruction to take a good look at the house emphasizes
the importance of examining the interior images. The
instruction is repeated after the invitation to enter a particular room. The choice of room will have a significance
for the imaginer. The allusion to smell points out that we,
in speaking of "images," often forget that we can also imagine smells, the taste of a dish, the feeling of touch.
Sounds can be heard as well. The vividness of images
increases with the number of senses involved. In guided
imagining, such pointers encourage the imaginer to take
seriously not only the visual but also the so-called "mundane" image sensations.

The question referring to meeting a person or seeing an
object encourages admission of encounter in general, possibly even confrontation, or allowing an object connected

with memories, one perhaps not thought about for a long time, to rise back into consciousness with its attendant chains of association, stories and feelings.

The instruction to rebuild the house points to a possibility inherent in the imagination: even something that seems like a perennial given may be "rebuilt," and it is possible to look at the result of this reconstruction to see whether the house then really is more appropriate to our needs. The directive relates to the imagination's ability to open up things.

The house in which one would like to live addresses the level of wishes, one we encounter time and again in our imagining. This wish level strikes me as very important: frequently we do not know what it is we really wish for, we just feel discontented—or else we no longer wish for anything in life, which means that we have lapsed into a state of resignation. In order to actively shape our lives we need our wishes as they are reflected in our imagination. It is another question whether they can be realized, or in what form.

The fantastic, utopian house opens up the imagination's surreal dimension, showing that it can move far from reality but also how far from reality an imaginer dares to go.

The image suggestion "house" is an intrinsically concrete stimulus of tremendous density, and I consider it particularly suitable for revealing various possibilities contained in the imagining. The childhood house connects us effortlessly with the story of our childhood. The further directions point out the road from the childhood house to the house of one's own wishes and thus encourage us to consider the development of our own autonomy within the space in which our ego lives its life.

Houses are spaces that provide us with the security in which we cultivate our relationship to our interior world and persons close to us. This imagining encourages us to take a look at how these spaces are represented in our interior images, how they can be formed and transformed.

Finally, the house always serves as a symbol of our personality, in a most comprehensive way.[29]

In providing a motif for the imagination, we stake out an image realm into which we may coax the imaginer's own images and make her demonstrate with which images she reacts. A proposed motif never addresses only one particular sphere. In most cases, these motifs are of great symbolic density.

In some procedures involving continuous image therapy such motifs are described in fairly unambiguous terms, even in regard to their meaning.[30] Other schools of thought insist that imaginative procedures should be based solely on motifs rising out of the imaginer's own unconscious, that no restrictions should be imposed on the autonomy of the unconscious, and that the contents animated in the unconscious should determine the course of the imagining, unhampered by prescribed motifs. Naturally, anyone working with imaginings in a general therapeutic context, i.e., not conducting imagination therapy in a stricter sense, will use dream images or images that present themselves to the therapist in transference. But, for the very beginning of work with the imagination, it may be useful to employ a symbol that has collective significance and thus evokes responses in everybody.

When working with these processes in a group it is necessary to start out with such motifs.

Incidentally, the process of imagining based on a predetermined motif is not all that far removed from certain projective tests. In some story-telling tests, e.g., TAT and ORT,[31] the subject is shown plates depicting situations in a partially diffuse manner, thus asking her or him to complement perception with imagination. The subject is asked to come up with an idea of what is represented on the picture in question and to tell a story about it, making this as dramatic as possible. The test pictures are designed to encourage the subject to get involved with specific themes which have been clearly defined by the authors of the tests. However, even in these pictures everyone but the authors themselves will see his or her images as well. When we speak of "imaginings with motifs," we do not refer to such a ready-made picture but to an image which the imaginer can easily translate into an interior image.

Example: The Tree Motif

The tree motif is another one well suited to guided imagining. After a brief period of relaxation, the following directions may be given:

Imagine a tree or several trees . . .
What are the surroundings of the tree?
What is the weather like?
Look closely at the tree.
What does it look like?
Can you touch it, how does it feel?
Can you smell it?
Are there other people approaching the tree?

First of all, the tree is a natural object, but it is also more than that. It is a symbol. It can stand for aspects of our humanness and express them. Even the kind of tree we see, the tree we are in a sense choosing from among all possible trees we know, says a lot about ourselves. There is a difference between a preference for an evergreen or an oak, the sense that an evergreen or an oak is "our tree" and thus represents a part of our nature. The evolution of a person is often compared to the growth of a tree. Having grown, we stand in the world like a tree—more or less well rooted, sturdy, and perhaps inflexible, or pliant and perhaps too easily swayed or bent in a storm. We may spread out like a treetop, bear fruit, then retire and regenerate; as a tree lives through its seasons, we live through the cycles of our lives. The way we have grown up in our particular manner, the way we stand in the world, may be expressed in the symbol of a tree.[32]

The landscape in which our imaginary tree stands tells us where we have settled in the world at this point in our life: perhaps on a hilltop, clearly visible to all, a good place for others to meet—or perhaps hidden away, behind a house, perhaps bearing fruit no one is really supposed to see.

The weather is an expression of our present emotional state. If we place the tree in a season that does not correspond with the actual time of year, this tells us about the season of our lives. In imagining, trees do not necessarily conform to their concrete characteristics: thus an oak may well bear apples, or one half of an apple tree may be in bloom while the other half is bare.

In most cases, we can easily translate images of this nature into terms of our actual lives, being intuitively aware of the events in our lives that might be connected with such an image. The image may also give rise to a new hope. This is the case with the above-mentioned apple tree, an image created by a woman whose husband died a little over a year ago and who tends to think of her psyche as a wasteland: the image points out to her that feelings of spring are also present again.

This exemplifies what always becomes apparent in work with images: our images always say something about ourselves, they always refer to ourselves, but they may also add to the image by including factors of which we are not yet conscious, and thereby bring about a change in our moods and energy levels.

The questions regarding tactile and olfactory perception are intended to stimulate other imaginative modes besides the visual. The question about other people raises the theme of encounter.

The tree symbol is particularly suited for a consideration of context: no tree stands in airless space, nor does
any human being. At the same time, the tree symbol stimulates the creation of images from very deep layers when
these are addressed. From time immemorial, the tree is
also a symbol for the growth of humanity as a whole. The
world tree, the world ash Yggdrasil, represents all hu-
mankind. Thus this motif in particular permits the creation
of images that extend far beyond personal self-image.

In general, it is worth considering that most motifs,
especially if they have a certain symbolic density, always
have a concomitant archetypal aspect and thus touch a
universal human theme in our psyche.

Technique

In learning the technique of imagery, guided imaginings
prove valuable for persons who do not use their imagination spontaneously. My pointers for the training of imaginative faculties are, of course, addressed to people who
are not spontaneous imaginers yet have the wish to establish closer contact with interior images and the transformation processes connected with them.

Guided imaginings lower the anxiety threshold of the
imaginer and facilitate his or her efforts to get in touch
with the images.

By means of diverse questions asked during guided
imagining, imaginers learn what questions they themselves may address to their images. When the imaginer no
longer needs such assistance, it may be discontinued, and
the therapist henceforth acts only as a companion who
intervenes when it seems necessary to do so.

The projected goal is a state in which imaginers deal
independently with their imaginings and use these even
outside the therapeutic situation, just as most people do
when they imagine situations they look forward to or

ones in which they have to stand their ground, as in an unpleasant argument.

Guided imaginings in which additional motifs that relate to the dynamics of the illness are suggested may prove very helpful, as for instance in the therapy of people suffering from depression[33] or others with functional, i.e., physical ailments for which no organic cause can be found.

Even with people who are rather at the mercy of these interior images, whose lives are determined by them—people who have insufficiently coherent ego complexes and hence find it hard to distinguish between interior and exterior, between what really is part of them and what isn't and thus easily lose touch with themselves, become confused, lose their sense of orientation in regard to themselves and others—carefully guided imagining may help them deal with such flood-like contents of their unconscious and enable them to establish boundaries. In the best-case scenario, such persons adopt the therapeutic method as a model for a way to deal with themselves; in the worst case, they will not be able to use the imaginative technique, or use it only when assisted by a therapist.

In my experience, spontaneous imagining need not always be chosen over the guided kind. Guided imagining may bring the imaginer into emotionally closer contact with the images. It is true that the imagining itself becomes more complicated in the guided technique: therapists may interrupt the process by interventions which may not always serve the image flow well, or exercise too great an influence on the client's process by their own images. Such eventualities have to be discussed between the imaginer and the therapist. Whenever we enter into a close therapeutic relationship, we exercise influence on each other both on a conscious and an unconscious level. We create something like a collective unconscious.[34] Thus it has to be assumed that we always influence each other with our images, and while this may be invigorating, it may also cause interference. Even when this subject is not discussed during imagining therapy, that influence exists whether interventions are used to a greater or lesser extent. The more we use interventions and motifs from which we expect essential change in the actual process, the more conscious and critical we have to be of both our procedure and our interventions.

The Flow of Interior Images

CHAPTER SIX

> One concentrates one's attention on some impressive but unintelligible dream-image, or on a spontaneous visual impression, and observes the changes taking place in it: a method (devised by myself) of introspection for observing *the stream of interior images*. [35]

JUNG'S PREMISE is that the interior images are in flux, and may be experienced as such. Many therapists have made the same observation.

On the other hand, we have repeated reports of fixed images which correspond with an emotional state of fixation on a problem or situation, and which are impervious to the possibility of being opened up by the abilities of our imagination. In rarer cases, the fixed images may point to the fact that they have to be questioned about their meaning just as they are, in their very immutability. More frequently, such solid-state images are connected to anxieties of some kind.

It appears certain that maximally vivid imaginings have the best therapeutic effect[36] when combined with a good deal of ego control. Vividness requires images in flux as well as a diversity of sensory modalities—one needs to produce images that are not only seen but also heard, smelled, that cause the heartbeat to accelerate, etc. Hence, everyone who uses imaginings in a therapeutic process is interested in setting images "in motion" so that they can be experienced. With people whose interior images don't flow, or who are worried that they might not do so, one can encourage confidence in the interior image flow by offering them an imaginative motif that contains the notion of flow to a high degree, e.g., water.

Example : The Water Motif

Possible directions for imagining (after light relaxation):
Imagine water.
If the water moves, follow its course, observe the water, the surroundings through which it flows or in which it rests.
Also observe the weather.
What feeling does this water evoke in you?
Where are you in the image?
Where is the water flowing?
If the water you see is a still water, remain calmly by this water, observe the water, the surroundings, and yourself.

Quite different forms of water may be seen, such as a brook, a river, a rivulet, springs, wells, a lake, the ocean, etc.

It goes without saying that each one of these various manifestations of water may be taken as a motif on which to exercise the imagination and experience the "psychic flow." I prefer to speak about water in general, in order to permit the expressive powers of the psyche as much autonomy as possible, but also in order to receive a diagnostic clue: our psyche represents itself differently when it depicts itself in images of a bubbling spring from when it sees itself by the ocean shore. In both cases, great interior vitality may be expressed, either in the experience of finding oneself next to the spring or perhaps even of being a spring of vitality oneself, a spring that can be viewed and possibly dealt with; or, in the case of the ocean, one may see oneself as a part of the mysterious source of life, of being, that exceeds us by far, that pulls us into the infinity of existence, into the very large rhythms in which we, too, participate.[37]

Naturally, the water motif is embedded in an environment. The observation of the surroundings permits the alternative of either basing one's images on memory or on imaginary surroundings. Most frequently, memories concern natural surroundings and feelings, problems, joys associated with them.

The question about one's own location in the image refers to the fact that it is possible to perceive this in different ways. One may see images and remain the person who sees these images without becoming truly aware of this. One may see images and include oneself in them, or one may identify with a protagonist in the image: thus, for instance, one may "become" the bubbling water, feel like bubbling water.

Water motif images are quite frequent even in spontaneous imaginings. This does not seem surprising if we consider how many water metaphors, images of water, we use when we express our psychic states. We may say that we "find ourselves at the source," we may "bubble over" with notions and ideas, but, before we know it, our "wellsprings" may have "run dry." When we are working, the "flow" may be good or interrupted; in the long "run," our life-flow may be suddenly "dammed up," we find ourselves "drying up," or else we find ourselves "going with the flow" again. But we may also be "washed out."

Often we use these images without really seeing them. If we did see them, we could get closer to the present psychic condition that expresses itself in them.

Water can be controlled by dams. We speak of "dammed-up anger." There are times when water appropriates things that do not really belong to it, are obstacles, and may pile up at a bend in the river. These "logjams" may have to be cleared, and we use the expression in such situations.

Water may also break its boundaries, cause floods, demolish dams, flood tracts we don't want to see flooded: an image of being destructively flooded by emotions which could otherwise be animating.

But we also speak of the "depths" of the psyche, and even this seems to reflect a water image—depth of water, depth of the psyche.

In this way, water images always express the actual emotional, psychophysical life and animation of our being, but also the way in which we psychically exist in the river of life, in the continuous transformation that bodies of water are particularly apt to render visible.

Hence, the water motif strikes me as more likely to stimulate our image flow than almost any other. In addition, the water motif also tends to call forth images containing sounds, all kinds of noises, smells, body experiences.

The image flow may, of course, also be stimulated by motifs like wind, storm, fire. However, the wind motif strikes me as more abstract, since its experience is always mediated—by, say, moving water, swaying trees, etc.; the fire motif, having a destructive aspect, is easily associated with fear.[38]

Moving images also result from motifs of moving animals or the travel motif.

Images from Literature as Triggers for Moving Images

Images conveyed by literature evoke images in the psyche of the reader. If they fail to do so, we feel that a text doesn't really engage us, we don't feel moved by it. While it may give cause for reflection, it doesn't animate us emotionally. There are texts that present us with the flow of their author's imagination, and this, in turn, stimulates the flow of the reader's imagination, particularly when the text stimulates him or her to really experience the described images with all senses.[39]

Our interior images are also stimulated by fairy tales told in a terse and pithy language that relies on images. When people begin to train their imaginative faculties, one may read them a fairy tale, or part of a fairy tale, with the suggestion that they try to see the images as vividly as possible. The advantage of reading an entire fairy tale lies in the fact that the imaginer knows the story will reach a happy ending and is hence able to endure even rather unpleasant images, since these are merely transitional.[40]

When we use fairy-tale images to introduce clients to imagery in motion, we also encourage them to generate fantastic images, symbolic creations that can no longer be located close to real life. They also make it possible to experience fantastic turns of event—at least this once—and such fantastic turns correspond to creative solutions in real life. The structure of the fairy tale—presentation of the problem, complications, solution—frees the imaginer from anxiety. Problems can be allowed in because we know there will be a solution to them.

In a more advanced phase it is possible to start out from fairy tale images that are particularly relevant to the imaginer to create spontaneous or guided imaginings. If the theme of a fairy tale concerns us, it is also a theme in our life. Relying on the images of the fairy tale we can reach parts of our psyche that cause difficulties but also contain developmental possibilities.

Example : "The Purple Flower"

Many colorful tales from the fairy-tale world are eminently suited to set our imaginings in motion. A particularly stimulating example is the Russian fairy tale "The Purple Flower." [41]

When I read only a section of a tale, I first tell my group, after relaxation, the beginning of the story; then I read the selected part, give a synopsis of the end, and ask the imaginers to recall, one more time, the images they found particularly enjoyable, disgusting, or astounding. After this, I direct them to detach themselves from the images, open their eyes, etc.

The Purple Flower

The story begins with a merchant setting out on a journey. The merchant has three daughters, and when he returns from his travels, he always brings them something they have asked for. The two older ones always ask for something tangible: a length of silk, cambric, and so on. But the youngest asks for a purple flower. Unfortunately, the merchant is unable to find such a flower. He returns home without it, and his little daughter is very sad. Twice he comes back without the flower, but this year, the third year, he leaves town[42] "and walked into the forest. He walked and walked, and the road through the forest went ever on.

"As he was walking along, he suddenly saw a garden. 'Hey, I'll go in and see what they have here.' He entered the garden: flowers as far as the eye could see! The air was wonderful, filled with the fragrance of flowers. Suddenly he saw the purple flower. He went over to it and picked it, but he had hardly touched it when he was scared out of his wits by an incredibly loud noise—and saw a horrifying monster flying right at him, and did not know what to do. The monster spoke to him: 'Well now, dear merchant, if you want to take that flower, I'll give it to you—but only in return for your daughter. I'll even throw in this ring, to please her. It's a plaything for her. Here, take the ring and give it to her, tell her to put it on her finger. Now go.'

"So the merchant took the flower and the ring and went to the ships that were all ready to leave, and they sailed away.

"When he returned home, he brought his daughters the things they had asked for—I can't remember what their wishes had been this time, they always asked for something else. He gave them their presents.

"The youngest asked him: 'Well, dear father, did you bring me anything?'

"And he said: 'I brought you the purple flower.'

"She was very pleased indeed. She started playing with the flower and kept asking him where it had grown, saying she'd like to go there herself. The flower spread all kinds of different fragrances. She kept asking questions:

"'Dear father, where is this garden where you found the purple flower?'

"'Oh, little one, it is far away, beyond many seas.'

"'Oh, father, I must see that garden.'

"But he thought: 'If I give her the ring, too, she'll know right away what kind of a garden it is.'

"And he held his peace and didn't give her the ring, yet.

"But then he thought: 'Well, why not give it to her, just to calm her down.'

"'Here, dear daughter, here's a ring, and now you can calm down for a year. When the year is over, I'll take you with me on a ship and show you the garden.'

"But as soon as she put the ring on her finger, she was instantly transported to that garden. She liked that a lot. 'But how did I get here?' she wondered. 'How lovely it is!'

"All around her there were flowers and lovely fragrances. And there was a palace there, too, shiny as if gold had been poured over it, and she felt so happy she didn't know what to do. She felt so good she didn't notice the passing of time at all. So this was where the purple flower grew. She spent a happy day in the garden, then went to the palace and found a sleeping chamber with a beautifully made-up bed with down pillows. There were carpets on the floor, mirrors everywhere—it was really splendiferous. She was overcome by weariness and fell asleep.

When she woke up, she went to a table set with wonderful food, and music was playing, and every kind of entertainment she could think of was at her beck and call.

"So she sat there and drank her tea and thought to herself: 'Who can this benefactor be who is taking such good care of me? I've got everything here I could ever wish for. I haven't had it this good even at home. So show yourself, lord of the manor, whoever you are!'

"All of a sudden she heard a voice: 'Listen, pretty Alexandra, I would very much like to show myself to you, but I know you'd be frightened of me. I'll grant you your every wish. I am the purple flower, but I do not dare show myself to you, for I am horrifying—you'd be frightened of me.'

"But she replied: 'No, go ahead, show yourself, my lord, I won't mind, I am not afraid of you.'

"'Well then, I'll do it to please you, I'll show myself—but watch out!'

"And suddenly there appeared such a horrifying monster that she fainted away in a swoon. At last she came to, and he asked her: 'Well, did you see me now?'

"'It's all right, my lord, it is good that you showed yourself to me. Now I won't be afraid of you anymore.'

"So Alexandra is happy again and has a lovely time, but then she gets homesick. With the help of her ring she can return home anytime she wants, but she must not stay longer than a week. Back home, she forgets that, but at last she remembers her promise to return to her purple flower. She returns to the garden, and she sees her lord, the purple flower in his arms, lying there dead and cold. She embraces him and cries out, in tears: 'Who will console me now? How can I go on living?'

"Then a great thunderclap is heard, and in front of her stands a marvelously handsome prince. He confesses to her that he is a son of the czar, that a spell had been cast on him, but now that she has embraced him, he is free of the spell. And they celebrate their wedding."

This tale consists of a multitude of images and sets a multitude of images in motion if we can and wish to deal with them.

When these archetypal images, concerning difficulties and their possible developments as they typically appear in human life and the unconscious, are enriched with personal material, the common human themes acquire a personal coloration.

Conversely, personal images may be related to these archetypal images and tied in with the symbolic processes inherent in them; this opens up ways for solutions that have not yet revealed themselves in the individual's imagination. While symbolic processes as expressed in myths and fairy tales may be operative within our actual existence, they simultaneously refer to a supra-individual, collective background: myths, fairy tales, and symbols inhabit an intermediary space that is a perennial space of imagination, creativity in general, and art.

To work on our imaginative abilities with fairy tales enables us to benefit, to a high degree, from the possibilities of a medium which in itself is an expression of the space of imagination, and to stimulate that space in ourselves. This, in turn, teaches us new possibilities for solutions.

Fairy tales also encourage us to employ solutions that are fantastic in the best sense of the word. In addition, we can and do learn from the fairy-tale hero or heroine how to find model solutions for certain problems expressed in the symbolic process: in the case of this tale, the fascinating relationship to the male and to sexuality. In the identification with the fairy-tale heroine we are taught how to deal with the terrifying in a courageous manner: "Now that I have seen you, I won't be afraid of you anymore."

Fairy tales contain descriptions of many strategies for our dealings with interior figures, and we can use them in our spontaneous imaginings.

Example from Therapeutic Practice

A woman's dream (age c. 35):

I am in a castle-like country mansion. Everything is mysterious, very beautiful but sinister as well. A little frightening. No one seems to be home. I walk from room to room, they are all nicely furnished, but there is no one there.

I feel more and more afraid . . . I wake up.

The analysand speaks of fear and also says that the dream seems very alien and unfamiliar to her. She can't provide many associations. The furnished but vacant rooms remind her of the fact that she herself keeps rooms furnished for guests who never show up. Her problem with loneliness is discussed, a problem with which she is quite familiar: in her dream it gains a sinister dimension, the surmise that something sinister, i.e., frightening, could be concealed in it.

The dream reminded me spontaneously of the fairy tale about the animal bridegroom, "The Purple Flower." In that tale, the heroine walks through a castle that is magnificently furnished but endlessly empty because no human beings are present. The eeriness can be experienced particularly in those versions of the tale in which invisible hands set piping-hot food on the table.

This example demonstrates that a motif for imagining, in this case an entire sequence of motifs, may be created out of an analyst's feeling of countertransference.

Excursus: Countertransference

Countertransference, as I understand it, consists primarily of the sum of the feelings the analyst has in regard to the analysand in an analytical situation, and that he or she tries to formulate in some way.

These feelings of the analyst may correspond exactly to the analysand's feelings, may thus provide direct access to these, and enable the analyst to achieve an empathetic understanding of the analysand.

However, we analysts often feel resistance against feelings that have been aroused in us by the analysand's feelings. In becoming empathetically aware of our resistance, we sense the nature of the threat; in most cases, this makes it possible for us to deduce the nature of the threat the analysand is experiencing.

Countertransference does not involve just emotions. We frequently have the impression of being pushed into a certain attitude, a certain role, against our will and against any therapeutic intention. This may well be, as Sandler points out,[43] the analysand's attempt to reestablish a relationship pattern that was once important and provided security in her or his life.

There also are countertransference emotions that express themselves as images, often archetypal images, i.e., symbols significant to everybody. In an archetypal countertransference, the analyst, reminded of symbolic material related to the analysand's situation, places that situation in a larger context.

In this case, my response to the analysand's dream with a section of a fairy tale is an example of this kind of countertransference.

In regard to all these aspects of countertransference, it is essential to understand them as expressions of the fact that the analysand's unconscious and the analyst's unconscious are communicating with each other[44]—that people are occasionally able to inspire an image in another person that expresses that person's situation very precisely and contains a possibility for further development.

I tell the analysand the initial phase of the tale and then read her a part of it, encouraging her to imagine the images as vividly as possible. She does this successfully: she can smell the fragrance of the garden as well as the odor of the monster. The castle is, by the way, identical with the castle in her dream.

Then I ask the analysand to re-imagine an image that has been particularly clear, an image that has the greatest intensity for her—and to let it change.

She imagines the horrifying monster: she sees a dinosaur with a crocodile's head, human eyes and eyeglasses, fiery breath; fire spews from nostrils and mouth. She sees the tale's heroine faint and revive again. The monster is simply there. Identifying with the heroine, she then tells the monster: "Now at least I know what you look like and that you won't devour me. Now I'm not afraid anymore."

She looks at the monster, establishes eye contact with it. "Whenever I look into its eyes it becomes smaller, that monster, and spews less fire. . . . But I can't stand it for long, and the monster can't stand it either, it goes away. By the way, I'm really in the house I saw in my dream, and what makes me feel so afraid is this monster. Now I know a little about how to deal with it."

This imagining took place in the fourth analytical session. The analysand is not familiar with imaginative technique but has a spontaneous command of it. Using the eyes and glasses as cues, we then tried to discover whose disguise this monster might be. A monster of this kind rarely represents a single person. In most cases, it combines various fear-inducing experiences in a person's life. Thus, in the case of this analysand, eyes and eyeglasses were derived from two different persons she had experienced as unequivocally fear-inducing authority figures.

The fairy tale taught the analysand that one must look at what frightens one; that it is possible to do so; that it then no longer generates such strong fear, and that one isn't simply at the mercy of the monster.

In order to set images in motion and to follow the interior image flow, we need to acquire strategies that enable us to react in frightening situations in a way that allows the images to continue, instead of being interrupted or frozen. Such strategies can be learned from extensive reading in fairy tales: they provide us with intuitive knowledge of what strategies might be situationally helpful. Or we experience with a therapist how he or she intervenes in the imaginative process, and then interiorize these intervention techniques so that we can later use them ourselves.

Fairy tales instruct us not only on appropriate behavior in dealing with frightening figures, they also teach us that one needs to be correctly prepared before going on a journey—and this applies to interior journeys of imagining as well. In fairy tales, to be correctly prepared means to have some good food and drink, sleep, and rest before taking the decisive step of a journey.[45] In the realm of imagination we take recourse to a few images of relaxation.

Images of Relaxation

CHAPTER SEVEN

I CALL IMAGES OF RELAXATION those images that we know are beneficial to us, relax us, and may return us to a certain state of well-being.

It is advisable to discover a few relaxation images for oneself or for other imaginers and then to practice these with some frequency.

Relaxation images do not necessarily involve the imagining of entire processes, although this is of course possible: more often it is a question of single images, quite frequently memories of situations in which we felt good or experienced a heightened sense of life.

Hence, these are mostly not particularly animated images but images that express and transmit calmness. I also call them images of calm.

Exactly because the flow of interior images is so important in imaginative therapy, the existence of the opposite pole should not be forgotten: not fixed images corresponding to fixed imaginings, but images that radiate a feeling of great calmness because they change very little or not at all.

Whenever imaginings are conflict-laden and put great strain on our emotions, a rest period in an image of relaxation may change the situation to a greater degree than the employment of other strategies for dealing with fear-inducing material.

Suggestion:
Imagine a situation in which you feel particularly good, have felt particularly good, or might feel particularly good.

Allow this image to become quite vivid, then imagine how this situation might change so that you would feel even better.

Enjoy the situation.

Examples from Therapeutic Practice

To demonstrate how different images of relaxation can be, I present these two, provided by two different analysands.

The first one comes from a forty-four-year-old man who suffers from states of depression. With him, the prominent problem is that he is not permitted to be himself, due to a deep fear that he might be "abandoned" if he were.

Biographically speaking, he was never truly abandoned as a child, but his needs and feelings were rarely noticed, and to that extent he often was abandoned. This feeling was combined with feelings of not being worth very much. His image of relaxation is the following:

I am dancing with abandon, I hear the music. It is rock. (I choose between rock and polka.) Today I choose rock music. I dance all by myself in the middle of a circle, I sense the moves of the others, they egg me on—we sweat, I smell the sweat, I feel full of strength—yet light. Then the whole group takes me into its arms, and a woman for whom I care a lot looks at me with a radiant face and says: "Your moves are great." Then I go to a pool to splash around . . . but the fantasy becomes less vivid there. I feel good, alive.

This image sequence that relaxes the analysand also strengthens his ego complex and his feeling of being himself; in his imagination, he is able to perceive himself very physically, to take pleasure in himself—and to accept himself, including the sweat which he otherwise avoids at any cost. In his aliveness he is also accepted by a larger group and admired by a woman who is very important to him. He feels physically alive and accepted, and this relaxes him.

In his image sequence he takes the risk of being himself, even putting himself in the center of things, and he is not abandoned—quite the contrary.

The relaxation images we choose often have to do with some fundamental problem of ours that we're trying to heal in our images. The fundamental problem is not abolished by this procedure, but it becomes possible to experience other and new emotional sensations.

The second image of relaxation was created by a forty-eight-year-old man, also a sufferer from depressive states. His case foregrounds guilt feelings: he lives with the impression of constant guilt. This causes his self-esteem to be very shaky, and he reacts to the slightest doubts expressed by others by feeling that he is a failure and doesn't really deserve to live. His image:

I am lying in a round pond, big enough to stretch out in. The water is pleasantly warm, like in a bathtub. I feel my skin with pleasure. I smell the grass, it must have been cut just a while ago. I feel very light in the water, the sun is shining on me. It is wonderful, no one wants anything from me, I don't have to do anything, I simply feel good.

This image sequence also supports the analysand's ego complex. He feels so good in his skin, he does not have to meet the needs of other people—he, who otherwise experiences the world as consisting of nothing but demands impossible to meet even when he musters all his energy.

His relaxation image is an image of security, calm, replenishment; by remaining in this pleasant warm water, somewhat reminiscent of amniotic fluid, he recuperates. These are images that belong to the nurturing aspect of the mother complex, images that permit a person to simply be, images that are sometimes even feared because they might seduce one to wallow in them, to let oneself be spoiled like a child by its mother, and to withdraw from the harsher aspects of life.

That danger is, of course, always present, but it is no reason not to consciously examine these relaxation images in order to discover what longings are expressed in them. When we perceive these consciously, there is also the possibility of employing them in a purposeful fashion when we need them.

When dealing with a few basic themes in our life, a few basic traumas and difficulties, it seems extraordinarily important to me to collect such images and to render them as vividly as possible.

Lazarus[46] uses imaginative therapy by presenting images which he thinks—probably even knows—are capable of influencing a person's basic problems in a positive direction. He thus establishes a direct connection between diagnosis and therapeutic imagining, especially in cases involving various functional disorders. It seems to me, however, that relaxation images analysands themselves provide are considerably more precise, and indicate more precisely which images and attitudes might change the themes of their basic problems, and the problems themselves, in their specific cases.

Images of Relaxation as Images of Longing

Images of relaxation may also be particularly effective in revealing longings when someone follows the suggestion to imagine a situation in which she or he would feel particularly good, and then to change that situation so that he or she will feel even better. The suggestion points out the possibility of creating images that do not correspond to concrete experience but are wishful images, images of our longing.

In this context, a question presents itself: Aren't all of these interior images wishful, and doesn't one make a person even more unhappy when one lets him or her imagine situations they will never be able to realize in their everyday lives?

I prefer to call these images images of longing, rather than wishfulness, since less prejudice adheres to such a term.

To even have wishes is often regarded as a sign of immaturity, of one's inability to make one's wishes come true. Freud's writings have strengthened this notion considerably. He says:

> The best-known productions of phantasy are the so-called "day-dreams," . . . imagined satisfactions of ambitious, megalomaniac, erotic wishes, which flourish all the more exuberantly the more reality counsels modesty and restraint. The essence of the happiness of phantasy—making the obtaining of pleasure free once more from the assent of reality—is shown in them unmistakably.[47]

And: "We may lay it down that a happy person never phantasies, only an unsatisfied one."[48]

Who would want to admit to one's wishes when these reveal one's life as a "life compelled to self-imposed modesty," thereby admitting to being frustrated?

Bloch[49] on the other hand, repeatedly stresses that the realm of imagination is the realm of wish and utopia. He also holds the opinion that the wish does not have a merely compensatory function, i.e., to make everyday life endurable, but that it is precisely the ability to have wishes, to create utopias, on which depends our special ability to "anticipate" the future and, thus, to relate our entire existence to new goals, new ideas.

This view of the imagination is widely held today.[50] Yet time and again one hears the question of whether our imaginings always merely depict our wishes, or whether they can be redeemed, as it were, by the gradual realization of these images in everyday life—whether they should be seen as castles in the air, or whether they truly represent interior energies that have not yet been brought to realization.

Whatever the value we assign to these images of longing, the fact remains that we do have wishes and longings. We make imaginative life projections and plan our future, be it because our present life still isn't what we imagine it could be, or be it that life, as long as it exists, never remains content, always pursues a longing anew, and keeps on giving birth to ideas that are not immediately identifiable as grandiose, castle-in-the-air notions that extend far beyond our true capabilities, or whether such supposed delusions of grandeur are containers of a secret knowledge of vital possibilities for the future that could indeed be realized. Very frequently these so-called grandiose ideas are generated by dynamic energies that may propel us out of mere passive tranquility.

In itself, the term "grandiose"—frequently used by others, not the person whose idea it is—does not mean much, characterized as it is by the worry that "a tree might grow as high as heaven" and mostly not devoid of envy. Every idea later proven creative has first presented itself as "grandiose"—only the results show whether it was or not.

Such ideas and images of longing arise out of a yearning for a better life. They are sustained by the role models of a person's own life as well as those of humanity at large. Images of longing, combined with the emotion of longing, are certainly capable of providing the ego with the energy to attempt to translate these images, at least partially, into reality.

We do, of course, all know people who spend their days and weeks expressing grandiose declarations of intent without any results whatsoever. I doubt, however, whether such people have been truly and emotionally engaged by images of longing. I tend to believe that they are the ones who resist any engagement, either by the demands of everyday life or by images of longing.

As in all human affairs, we may find here a possibility of degeneration, but this need not give all longing and its characteristic projective imaginings a bad name. The imagination always contains unredeemed future—a future that can be redeemed.

Our longings frighten us because we are afraid they might entangle us into a wish-world, entice us to set goals for our lives that we won't be able to achieve. This may of course happen, particularly if we believe that every longing has to be integrated into reality without modifications. The value of a utopia is not proven by its unmodified translation into everyday life but by how many of us that utopia has set in motion, and how much spiritual inspiration we, and others, have received from it. The world of imagination, of symbols, always has dimensions that resist simple translation into everyday life; they extend beyond our world, and their essential function consists exactly of their ability to propel us out of the mundane.

If we do not permit ourselves images of longing, we do not permit or grant ourselves a future. Above all, we deny ourselves the transformative energy that is expressed in these images.

When we truly abandon ourselves to such images of longing, they have a great influence on our mood: they trigger hope, hope for change, hope for something that will fit better into our lives, that makes our lives be more in tune.

It is for this very reason that images of longing may also be images of well-being, relaxation, refreshment: they renew the possibility of hope. But we do have to allow them in, engage them fully on the emotional level, allow them to move us. We can't just let them parade by our mind's eye like pleasant movies that really don't concern us personally. Only when images of longing are vivified will they change our moods, our further fantasies, our imaginings.

Thus it is not a question of avoiding these images of longing, but a question of immersing ourselves completely in them.

Seen this way, images of longing, images of relaxation, may indicate to us what images we need in order to deal more effectively with some fundamental difficulty.

Themes of Inhibition and Development

That themes of inhibition and development are always touched upon in our interior images becomes clear when we create a theoretical connection between our complexes, as understood by C. G. Jung, and our imaginings. Jung says that complexes develop a peculiar fantasy activity: in our sleep, the fantasy appears as a dream, but even in a waking state we dream on, below the threshold of our consciousness, due to "repressed or other unconscious complexes."[51] As early as 1916 Jung pointed to the emotionally determined contents from which imaginings (fantasy creations, sequences of images) and the formation of symbols arise. Complexes are energy centers built up around an affectively determined kernel of significance, presumably called into being by a painful collision between the individual with a demand or an event in his or her surroundings with which he or she has not been able to cope. Every subsequent event in that direction will then be interpreted according to this complex and reinforces it: the feeling-tone (the emotion) of which the complex consists, is preserved and even strengthened.[52] In this sense, complexes mark critically vulnerable spots in the individual's psyche. As energy centers they do, however, produce a certain activity—expressed in emotion—and the individual's psychic life then consists, to a great extent, of that activity.

The complex certainly contains much that blocks the individual's way to personal growth. On the other hand, complexes also contain "germs of new life and vital possibilities for the future."[53] These creative seeds become apparent when we accept the complexes and permit them to run the gamut of fantasy. We all have complexes: they are expressions of themes in our lives that also are problems in our lives. They shape our inescapable psychic dispositions. Thus, symbols and symbolic representations are expressions of complexes as well as the sites on which complexes can be processed.

While complexes indicate a theme of repression, they can also present themselves in a developmental theme, in an image of longing, or in smaller steps in new images that weren't previously possible. In the interior images, psychic energy is being transformed, made available to experience in new depictions. If, however, a complex is of great intensity, the repression theme will express itself dramatically, and the development theme will express itself by means of a grandiose fantasy that initially has nothing to do with moderate development. This is the case to an even higher degree when complexes charged with high energy drain energy away from the ego complex and thus threaten the ego: this threat is made more bearable, perhaps even neutralized, by means of a fantasy of being "important" or capable of important things.

In working with images it makes a great difference whether we work with notions of grandeur or with images of complexes representing the psychic situation and, in themselves, pointing to the future, but not at all as radically as the former wish-image does. If need be, such a wish-image may be understood as compensation by the complex constellation, or as compensation by the ego that has been made deeply insecure by the complex constellation.

It may also be observed that people whose ego is severely threatened, who are doing very poorly, are more likely to have fantasies of grandeur. Thus, fantasies of grandeur may be expressions of a very special creativity, a very special vision, but they may also indicate that a person's ego structure is brittle, either fundamentally or because that person is placed in a specific situation of psychic stress.

Even in such stressful situations, fantasies of grandeur may have a stabilizing effect on the imaginers. The very possibility of a notion of grandeur gives them the feeling that not everything is lost in their lives, and thus they regain the energy they need to free themselves from the pressure to which they are subjected.

If, on one hand, one were to ask these people to live up to their notions of grandeur, one would be asking too much of them—as, for instance, when someone in a difficult situation imagines a wonderful elephant and now feels he has to match this marvelous creature in everyday life. If, on the other hand, this person can tell herself that she is, despite her misery, capable of seeing and experiencing this image that arouses feelings of strength, calm, resolution, possible wildness, then she can embrace those emotions and face everyday existence in an altered state.

Generally speaking, I see a problem only if we identify with these notions of grandeur, hence put excessive demands on ourselves, and often no longer perceive other images also belonging to our psychic landscape, but restrict ourselves to one image or two.

The Relation of Images to Reality

Possible imagining instruction:
   Imagine a tree.
   Look at it closely, including its surroundings.
   Try to feel, for a while, as if you were this tree.
   Perceive your feelings.
   Now look at the tree again, from the outside.
   Then detach yourself from the image and imagine a tree you
   admire, a tree you consider really special.

The following imaginings were made by a fifty-four-year-old woman who suffered from diffuse functional digestive ailments. In our sixth analytical session I suggested we try the imagining method, hoping for further diagnostic clues for her case history.

I ask her to imagine a tree. She sees an araucaria, a conifer indigenous to Australia and South America. The tree can grow to a height of seventy meters and produces mealy seeds that are edible. Its wood is used in shipbuilding. The woman describes it: "The araucaria is tall, with wide branches, not too many, really wide-spread branches, one can see through them. I see a very slender trunk and dark-green needles; these needles are evergreen, quite dark, almost black. These needles are very important."

I ask her to imagine herself as that tree.

She experiences it: "I feel slender, taut, I rise up to the sky and feel really wide. I also have big roots, stretching wide. I stand alone. . . . " Now she becomes an observer again: "These trees are always solitary." Here she tells me something essential about herself.

Then I ask her to imagine a tree she admires, and she says: "But, well, that is a tree I admire, the araucaria."

Thus, she responds to the suggestion to imagine a tree

by imagining a tree she admires. I now ask her to imagine an ordinary tree.

She sees a handsome copper beech, tall, very old, very sturdy with a thick trunk, solid and protective.

I ask her to differentiate the two feelings. When you imagine two different trees, you may consider what feelings are brought up by one or the other.

Her reply: "The copper beech gives me this feeling: look down more, into myself; an urge to protect, to wrap up. I want to gather into my branches everything I love, everything that feels good with me. As a copper beech, I am not so alone, and that is much more enjoyable. With the araucaria I feel more of a pull skyward, I feel more transparent, permeable. I have the feeling I have to take everything into myself, to carry it upward."

Suddenly, the normal tree becomes an admired tree. When the normal tree becomes the admired tree, this may mean that the analysand always has to be ahead of herself, that she has no permission to be normal, has to be admired, and evidently even can be admired—she imagines a wonderful tree. It is the problem of staying ahead of yourself, or, in other words, the problem of an excessive demand, a continuous need to be validated. Functional digestive problems may be connected with excessive psychic demand—which may, of course, also serve as a stimulus. Now the question is: Does this woman have enough strength, or doesn't she, to meet the demand? In such a case it is, of course, important to know if the imaginer notices that she transforms the normal tree into an admired one. This woman realizes it as soon as I ask her to imagine a tree she admires. The next question is, does she devalue the normal tree; does she devalue the "normal," in this case the copper beech, which actually seems pleasant and very harmonious, because she wants something else there? Something spectacular?

In her own words, the araucaria expresses the feeling of being able to grow toward heaven, a feeling of being able to reach up into the realm of transcendence. This tree is also connected with a certain lightness, although it is well-rooted. But it stands alone. This "I stand alone"—in the identification with the araucaria—has triggered fear, and as a consequence—in order to master that fear—she has become an observer. The change from identification to observation is crucial. When too much fear occurs in our imaginings, we instantly take a step back, become an observer. Mostly this happens involuntarily. In terms of strategy, it is important to remember that we should take good care to notice when fear occurs.

In her actual life, this woman is not so alone. What is expressed here really isn't loneliness, but rather the demand to be able to endure life by oneself, perhaps in the sense of a courageous notion of grandeur which, in turn, is expected to receive admiration. In addition, there is a very respectable sense of growing in the world, but it is "normal"—nothing special. Nevertheless, this independent, free-standing araucaria of luminous and transcendental connections seems to presage a new form of existence for her later years. This involves a sacrifice of the symbiotic wishes, the wish to accommodate everything in oneself.

A thematic direction given to the client's imagining may stimulate a dialogue between images that are closer to the world of wishes and images that belong to concretely experienced reality. This dialogue may also reveal longings, both in the sense of their possible dangers of excessive demand, and in their main theme, which helps overcome a present life problem.

It seems essential to me not to discard images of longing too hastily as unrealistic, as illusions of grandeur, or castles in the air, but to help the imaginer get in touch with them so that they may take an effect, and a potential for hope may be incorporated in them.

The Self-Image Reflected in Various Motifs of Imagining

OUR IMAGES always refer to our actual situation, to memory, and to longing. This is particularly true about our self-images. These would be incomplete without the aspect of longing. Our images always tell us something about ourselves, about how we see ourselves and the world that belongs to us, that is, our world.

However, certain motifs are more stimulating to aspects of our self-image than others: various motifs on which images are permitted to form may result in an interesting momentary confrontation with oneself. Self-images are always snapshots, showing which images are important to us and our lives at the moment.

By means of an example, I want to demonstrate how certain motifs reflect different aspects of the self-image, without the intention to provide a complete phenomenology of the self-image. Besides, there may well be people in whom other motifs elicit better reactions. Furthermore, I want to show how the therapist may intervene to keep the images flowing, and how it is possible to arrive at an interior dialogue, a dialogue between different, possibly even contradictory self-images.

In regard to interventions, it is important to know that we, as therapists, accompany the other person's images by imagining the described images as best we can. We react, and intervene, out of our own imagining of these images. It is also conceivable that another person's image motifs wake up images in us that concern and preoccupy us a great deal. Then it may become difficult to achieve empathy with the images of the client. In such a case, one may communicate one's own image to the client, and this enables us to resume shared experience.

Possible Instructions for Imagining

You see yourself standing in a landscape.
What does the landscape look like?
What do you look like?

You see yourself standing by a body of water.

You see yourself as a tree, standing somewhere.
What kind of tree are you?
Where does it stand?

You see yourself as an animal.
What kind of animal are you?

If you were an island, what kind of island would you be?

Where is it?
Who is there besides you?
How are the connections to the mainland?
Imagine a stage.
On this stage you stand, twice, in different clothes,
and if you like, even in different costumes.
And each one of you now says a sentence to the other.

These instructions are intended to make the imaginer assume the position of an observer. One is required to look at oneself, create an image of oneself. Then, if one identifies with figures that appear, this provides an opportunity beyond observation—to open up oneself one more time, to feel identity even more strongly. The instruction leaves that possibility open. In brief, the motifs may concern the following aspects of human existence:

The *landscape* motif, very frequently combined with an experience of the weather, shows where we place ourselves at the moment, and our predominant mood.

Water points to the momentarily present dynamics of the psyche. It shows what moves our psyche, or what it concentrates on. It may also let us know how and where we find ourselves in the river of life.

The *tree* demonstrates our state of growth in the world. It is a very immediate self-portrait: how would we be if we had to depict our existence by means of the tree motif?

The *animal* shows our vital, instinctive, even brutish side. The tree gives hardly an indication of this.

The *island* addresses itself to our depending-only-on-ourselves aspect, and naturally also to the question of social connections, relationships.

The *stage* motif animates images of what is on the playbill right now. The instruction to see oneself as two separate figures on stage touches on possible opposing elements of the self-image which may lead to conflicts. On the other hand, two complementary figures may appear.

This list is not intended to set interior images in motion but to help the therapist to remember to reflect upon him- or herself from different perspectives.

Example from Therapeutic Practice

A forty-four-year old therapist, who is learning the imagery technique, feels uninspired and asks me to simply give her a few motifs.

I give her the ones I have collected over the years which I consider likely to show essential aspects of the self-image.[54] These are the results:

Landscape: "I see myself in a very green landscape, it could be Ireland. I stand there in Wellington boots, legs wide apart. Behind me are hills, green hills shrouded in mist. In front of me is the open sea. I feel secure in this landscape."

Water: "I stand by the Danube. The river is low, but there is a current. It gives me a sense of calm, a calm flowing-by. I walk upriver and sense a pull."

Tree: "I am an evergreen. I feel elated, there must be a wind. Very lightly, my branches touch a copper beech standing close by. There are other trees, small beeches, small evergreens, a Norway spruce. I feel well rooted and very light. I have grown well, without towering above the others, but I am well formed, with strong branches. My needles are green, even though I have the feeling it really is autumn. Lovely, sunny weather in a cool season. I really like being an evergreen, so independent, light, and firm, and I even like this possibility of tenderness."

Animal: "I hesitate: I'd like to be a mountain lion, even see myself as feline, strong, slim. But I also want to be a piglet, about a week old: warm, rosy, alive, full of rollicking joie de vivre. Right now, I see one, rolling around . . ." This is where I intervene: "A piglet or a kitten?" She says: "A piglet . . . best of all, I'd like to be kitten-piglet. I see this piglet dashing about, squealing with pleasure, and I'd like to pick it up and hold it. Now I see how it sticks its snout into everything, how terribly curious it is. From the kitten, I want its playfulness and the softness that invites one to stroke it. Now I see the kitten-piglet, shaped like a piglet, its nose and mouth are those of a pig, but it has the fur of a kitten, cat's eyes and cat's paws. The kitten-piglet is able to move like a piglet or like a kitten."

Island: "I want to be an island in the Atlantic, with steep cliffs. Hidden behind those cliffs lies a green meadow, and there is an accessible sandy beach, also hidden, where one can cast anchor safely as long as one knows where. I want to be an island visited by people who want to reflect on things. I want to make this possible for them, simply by the way I am situated, the way I look. To reach me, you need a boat and brisk seas. It is also possible to fly in by helicopter, but I find that very unpleasant. It is a violation from the air. I enjoy being an island that exists for people who want to reflect on things."

Stage: "I'm having a little trouble. There is a small girl, there is a maternal woman, there is a brazen hussy, one very elegant in an evening gown slit at the side, one in dirty jeans who just dashes about the stage looking for something, one wrapped up from head to toe, one who'd like to show herself off in a bikini.

"I like the one in the evening gown, let her take the stage. It's a 1920s gown, deep décolletage, bare back, small stylish hat, good legs. She acts both licentious and decorous. I'm having a lot of fun describing her. She looks elegant but is rather vacuous. . . ."

Here I intervene and ask: "Who says that?"

"The one with the dirty jeans. You can tell she's been gardening, making healthy salads, she's probably solved all the riddles of the world, she doesn't care about appearances, she wants to be on top of things without pretense, she goes to a lot of trouble. She says to the woman in the evening gown: 'You're wasting your time in the world of appearances.'

"And the woman in the evening gown says: 'And you just stay glued to the earth's crust.'

"The one in jeans is visibly discouraged, thinks to herself: 'Useless to enter into an argument with her, she'll always have an answer.'

"Then I ask her: 'Aren't you afraid you'll wake up some day and feel yourself enslaved by the world of appearances?'

"The one in the evening gown says: 'No, why should I be? I'm not enslaved by the world of appearances. I dress like this when I feel like it, and at other times I wear different things.'

"The one in jeans says: 'But the people must be talking.'

"The one in the evening gown: 'People are always talking. They'll talk about your jeans.'

"The woman in the evening gown is firmly perched on a barstool, the one in jeans runs around the stage, irritable, then asks: 'What did you mean when you said I'd stay glued to the earth's crust?'

"And the woman in the evening gown says: 'What I meant was just that you don't go down into depth and don't make great plans, but you're decently trying to do what is at hand, lacking courage for anything extravagant. After all, I can always put on jeans, but can you put on an evening gown?'

"The woman in jeans asks: 'Do I have to be able to do that?'"

I notice that the imaginer is in some distress and tell her to go back to the director's space and find two people familiar to her, ask them for help, and she brings in her parents and says:

"My mother likes the woman in jeans a lot, and so does my father—he says so, at least, but he is looking at the one in the evening gown."

Then she takes her partner, a friend, to the director's space and considers who likes which woman better.

I tell her to invite someone she doesn't know on-stage, either another couple or a woman, a man.

She says: "Yes, here I come, sportily casual. The earth-crust jeans woman withdraws, and the evening gown woman takes her leave."

Spontaneously, these images evoke emotions and considerations, but they may also be interpreted by gathering additional associations.

This was the imaginer's spontaneous reaction: "I like the kitten-piglet best of all, I was really able to see it in my imagination. The image of the island was very strong, too. Then it was important for me to experience, in the stage image, the reason why I always have this dichotomy between the seductive woman who wants to be indolent and the other one who is so robust. I didn't know that that had to do with my father problem, but I can really see it now. And I'm a bit proud of the evergreen tree, I do like myself like that. Maybe I'd just like to be an evergreen, as an ideal image. I can't always be as light and full of life as I experience evergreens as being."

About the image of a landscape this woman says she feels secure in the green, somewhat mysterious Irish countryside. She herself makes a connection between herself in that image—in Wellington boots—and the woman who wears jeans: that is what she is like. Ireland is a memory image: a short while ago, she vacationed there with her family. It would, of course, be possible to add many more associations to these images, connected by the imaginer to persons with whom she has had relationships and who are present in her memories. Here, however, I want to restrict myself to the central aspect of this imagining, the one that concerns her self-image.

In the images related to the landscape motif she shows herself as a woman who has found a place in the world where she feels secure. She stands solidly on the ground, won't be easily unbalanced—and her feet will stay dry.

Her movement upstream, against the current, is what strikes one in her vision of the Danube; the current, however, is weak, and thus it is not hard to move against it. She was raised near the Danube and is surprised at how little water there is in her imagined Danube. This Danube of her imagining reminds her of a tributary of the Tiber that carried so little water one could wade across with ease.

At the time, she does not feel particularly "in motion," psychically—and yet the image tells her she is going against the flow, against her interior dynamic. This image corresponds best with her actual mood: she feels unenthusiastic. The tree relates to a more durable aspect of her self-image than the perennially moving water.

She says she always sees herself as an evergreen when asked to imagine herself in the shape of a tree, and admits that she has a particular fondness for that tree: a conifer that participates in seasonal changes. She stresses that other people, as well, assign this tree to her. What fascinates her about it is its elegance, lightness, airiness—combined with strength. She says she doesn't really know if she has already become a bit like the evergreen—she must have, otherwise people wouldn't see her in that shape— or if she is in the process of becoming more and more like it. For her, this tree is clearly an image of longing; she does not know how realistic or realizable it may be.

The copper beech connects her to her husband. This image says that she is proud of herself, of the existence into which she has grown; it indicates good self-esteem. It also becomes obvious that she is engaged in many and various developed relationships.

Speaking of the mountain lion, it occurs to her that she regards the mountain lion as a particularly vigorous, elegant cat. In reality, she has never seen a mountain lion. She goes on to say that she likes cats a great deal because they are elegant and tender yet very independent, doing as they please. She regards the mountain lion as a particularly dignified cat. In retrospect she thinks it may also have been a bit of an image of grandeur. Piglets and kittens, she says, are really much closer to her and depict a greater number of aspects of herself.

The piglets remind her of wartime experiences. When she was a small girl, her grandmother took her to visit a farm where a sow had just farrowed. The farmer put a piglet in her arms, and she stroked as if it had been a kitten. She finds the piglet particularly sweet.

Then there is one of her first memories: grandmother looks at her radiantly, gives her a kiss and says, "What a little piglet you are." She remembers this scene as an out-of-the-ordinary show of affection. She combines it with the piglet she had thought so sweet she would have liked to take it to bed with her.

"Kitten" is an affectionate nickname her husband often uses in regard to her. She likes it but knows that it describes only one side of her nature.

The self-image expressed in the animal is characterized by the aspects her grandmother and her husband have chosen to love in her. The question also arises whether her husband is sufficiently able to respond to what her grandmother called into life in her. The woman herself is primarily aware of the erotic and sexual playfulness in both animals.

Pig and cat are animals of the Great Goddess, who is, among other things, also the Great Mother—here we find the cross-connection to Grandmother. The pig is the animal sacred to Mother Goddess Demeter: it symbolizes her fertility, and thus is a symbol of good fortune.

Depending on whether they are domestic or wild, cats are beholden to the Egyptian goddesses Bastet and Sakhmet who appear in the shape of cats or lionesses or have them pull their chariots. The choice of these creatures to describe her animal aspect makes it very clear that the imaginer finds herself in a phase of life in which development of the feminine, and identification with the animal-feminine in all its erotic and sexual playfulness, have become important. At the same time, a longing becomes evident for a relationship like the one communicated to her by her grandmother. The animals are seen in their young, playful form: thus it is still a question of a beginning stage, although this also expresses a longing for the carefree state of youth.

The mountain lion would seem to be the goal, but its image does not reflect the imaginer's experience of the present moment.

The island image demonstrates that the imaginer is also quite capable of showing a brusque side, but if one knows how and when to reach the island, one is rewarded with a magnificent sandy beach. A great deal of softness and tenderness lies hidden behind a rather brusque manner of self-presentation—which somewhat contradicts the idea of being an evergreen. This brusqueness may be related to her feeling rather helpless when threatened from the air.

But she also knows—or hopes—that people are able to find themselves, to think things over when they are in her company, just because of the way she is, perhaps even because of her outwardly brusque appearance. This also means that she is capable of defending her boundaries, while being able to offer a sandy beach and green meadow in her hidden realm. But she is unprotected against threats from above.

At the onset, the stage motif inspires numerous visual notions, and a few new aspects become visible. At first, she does not want to settle for just two figures. When we consider how she has conflated piglet and kitten into kitten-piglet, a very creative neoform with which she is still able to identify, we may assume that she is momentarily less inclined toward conflict-laden analysis than toward integration.

She decides to concentrate on the woman in the evening gown and the one wearing jeans. Clearly, they embody two important sides of her. She says about the "jeans woman" that she is very familiar: that is her rough and ready side, a person of no illusions, so proud when she has done a good job gardening and providing healthy salads for her family, yet also quite skeptical as to whether there is such a thing as healthy salad. She doesn't make life easy for herself.

At the moment, she is more fascinated by the woman in the evening gown: "She exudes a certain disreputableness, eroticism, sexuality; she doesn't care about tomorrow, about the consequences of her actions; she is independent. In my twenties, I completely missed that sort of life. I wore nothing but jeans and was ideologically convinced that a woman could do a man's job, that all that 'seductiveness' was simply dishonest."

The lines those two then fire at one another make good sense to her. She says she's afraid to lose herself to that certainly fascinating world of appearances, but is also afraid to remain stuck to the earth's crust. But then, the woman in the evening gown turns out to be quite superior—she makes it clear that the gown is not her skin, that she does not identify with the persona of a woman of the world, but that she may wear such outfits whenever it amuses her to do so. She represents herself as the one who has more possibilities in life, and the courage to do something extravagant. The two figures are able to manifest themselves but insist on rejecting each other.

The intent of my intervention is to create a shift in the balance of power by introducing new figures into the scene. It is motivated by my sense that the conflict is becoming too painful and hence should not be left unresolved.

The imaginer produces figures to evaluate these two sides of her. She seems to want an either-or resolution, and also wants to see how the two figures are perceived and accepted by the outside. This results in the interesting revelation that her father was always verbally rooting for the jeans woman but emotionally would probably have preferred a woman of the world. This, too, may be a reason, as she herself points out, why she doesn't know which side to favor, and generally has the impression she has to choose one side and reject the other.

It takes another intervention to bring about a resolution—perhaps too quick a resolution. She walks on stage herself, "sportily casual," having integrated a bit from both women, and this makes it possible for the two to take their leave.

The images evoked by these motifs have showed diagnostically essential aspects of her self-image, but they have also moved her to analyze herself in an entirely new way.

The sequence of images also demonstrates how memories, actual experiences, and images of longing shade into one another, and how images of longing may also be experienced as such.

Pointers for Interpretation

CHAPTER NINE

LIKE DREAMS, imaginings can be interpreted. But, like dreams, they also have their effect without interpretation, as long as they are experienced and perceived as vividly as possible.

Especially in the case of motif imaginings, there is often a need to comprehend the images, the symbol-shaping processes. In interpretive processes, as in the interpretation of dreams,[55] we collect the imaginer's ideas about individual images and relate them to the imaginer's life situation. The symbols may also be connected with their collective meaning—the meaning they have had throughout human history, in forms in which they have been handed down to us: myths, fairy tales, art, the history of religion, etc. This places the images into a larger human context. An interpretation becomes particularly satisfying when its subject is experience within the analytical relationship that can actually be experienced right then—and is simultaneously made manifest in a symbol; when both actual experience and image reveal a connection based on life history, and also allow one to see the general human context. It is this embedding of the symbol in the great contexts of life that opens new perspectives of experience and understanding.

In the case of imaginings that extend over a long period, resulting in a story, it seems sensible to defer interpretation until the story has completed itself. On the other hand, interpretations may be useful whenever imagining comes to a halt for an extended period.

The Ego's Ability to Control in Regard to Interior Images

CHAPTER TEN

How to Stop Negative Images

QUITE FREQUENTLY, we make negative statements or have negative notions about ourselves. Often these statements are not introduced into our communication with others, they are usually used in conversation with ourselves. They say things like: I am nothing; I will be nothing; it would have been best if I hadn't been born; we can't do anything about things; they will always run right over us; etc. Many times we aren't even fully conscious of these evaluations; they simply affect our consciousness and change our mood. Then, this altered, discouraged, or resigned mood makes us see the world in even darker hues, and our chances of dealing with it seem even more hopeless—whereupon the world assumes an even more threatening character.

If these self-devaluing statements are seen as images, they're experienced even closer to the ego and may prevent us from using our imagination. Instead of enabling us to try out new modes of behavior, or to experience our-

selves in our ability to get ahead of our lives in our imagination, imagining becomes a tool used to really under-
mine our self-esteem. This always indicates that an interior
figure, mostly one representing a complex, has been given
a great deal of power over the ego complex, and the dialogue between the ego and the interior images has been
disrupted.

It does, therefore, make sense to learn how to deal with
interior images that strike us as negative in such a way
that we can put an end to them, and that we, from our ego
base, retain or attain a certain degree of control over these
images. When we're able to stop them, we're also able to
deal with our destructive notions. The stopping of images
that serve only to diminish and devalue the ego is a technique particularly developed by behavioral therapists.
They work on their clients' behavior by encouraging
them to imagine a step-by-step approach to the behavior
they wish for. In this process, relaxation plays a very
important part, and the individual imaginative steps are
based on a subtle analysis of behavior. These imaginings
are also practiced at home. In this kind of procedure it is,
of course, important to keep on imagining the desired
behavior, and not to let a sudden notion caused by fear
reveal the imaginer's shortcomings.

Cautela has described a "self-control tryad":[56] using it,
clients were able to reduce negative thought processes
and partially replace them with positive ones. The self-
control tryad consists of a combination of thought-stop-
ping, relaxation, and covert reinforcement. As soon as the
imaginer notices that his or her images are becoming negative, he or she is told to shout "stop" or to imagine a large
stop sign and relax her- or himself by means of deep
breathing. This is followed by "covert reinforcement," i.e.,
imagining a pleasant scene.

The individual steps are practiced and learned, and
according to Cautela they can be used "anytime and any-

where," eyes open or closed, whenever fear or negative thinking occurs, while driving, conversing, being tempted to overeat, etc.[57]

The self-control tryad is, indeed, helpful. In a psychoanalytical context, we'll use it in slightly modified form. The command to "stop" is used in the way suggested by Cautela; it is left to the individual's imagination whether he or she sees a stop sign or a red light or whatever else is made to represent this "stop."

Then he or she is asked: "What is it about this situation that confuses you so? Who is it who makes such negative statements about you? Take a close look."

After that image is perceived, the client is asked to relax physically by means of deep breathing. A relaxation image may also help the imaginer achieve equilibrium again.

At this point, in the non-imagining state, there usually follows a discussion about how to deal with this figure, what strategies might become necessary, what these negative images mean.

There are, however, images experienced as negative that should not be changed but looked at and accepted. They should be stopped only if there is an escalation of these negative evaluations and if they concern the client's self-image.

Example from Therapeutic Practice

A talented student has a tendency to suffer from great exam anxiety. Knowing this, he has prepared himself very well for the exam. He knows himself and his problem. But he has the impression that he'll never amount to anything.

I ask him to imagine the exam situation and this "never amounting to anything."

"I see myself in the exam situation, I'm sweating, sweat is pouring down my whole body, my beard is growing, I am already pale, and the black beard I'm growing makes me appear even paler, downright waxen. I start shrinking. My clothes get too large for me, and the sweat keeps on pouring."

I intervene: "Now stop!"

I ask him to breathe in and out deeply. Then I tell him: "Now imagine who it is who makes you shrink like that."

"Strange," he says, "it's a magnificent peacock. It spreads its tail in front of me, turns around, lets me admire it."

The image makes him laugh. The laughter, in turn, causes him to suddenly revert to his original size and to ask himself how on earth he could have thought he would not pass this exam. Clearly, his demand on himself does not have to be preening quite so blatantly.

When we stop negative images—and we should stop them only when their negativity escalates—when there no longer is a possibility of correction in the realm of imagination, this doesn't necessarily mean that the negative images will be simply replaced by positive ones, as in the above example.

If, in a therapy situation, negative images are stopped, it often happens that the imaginer first of all produces a pleasant image—for the therapist's benefit, as it were. But the very fact that she or he is able to see a positive image is bound to change the mood and break the destructive circle.

Even when no constructive images can be experienced, it is helpful to know that negative images can indeed be stopped—that we aren't simply at their mercy.

It is true that we're already stopping our negative thoughts as soon as we try to perceive them as images: these horrify us and make us aware of their destructiveness, and we are more inclined to let them go than when we devalue ourselves into a grandiose sacrifice in a half-unconscious, self-torturing fashion that is mildly enjoyable yet also very painful.

In my opinion, the negative images may also change because, in therapy, another human being tells us to make a halt here because he or she affectionately makes sure that this person afflicted by bad notions relaxes, perhaps even suggests an image of relaxation that makes him or her feel good. This makes it possible to experience an atmosphere of acceptance and safety, and this experience, in turn, affects the images.

How to Regard Negative Images

It may also happen that the imaginer stops the images experienced as negative and wants to replace them with a positive one without recognizing the significance of the images, but also without devaluing his or her self-image even more. There are certain aspects of ourselves we don't want to accept, don't want to "see." This may manifest itself as a blurring of the interior images so that they become unrecognizable—or we do still recognize them, but no longer find words or any other mode of expression for them, even when we normally don't find it all that difficult to translate the language of images into spoken/written language.

Example from Therapeutic Practice

A forty-five-year-old man imagines a tree: "It's a fine pear tree, close to my parents' house. It is tall, straight, but bare. Bare! The other trees have leaves, mine doesn't. I try to see another tree: an oak, up on a hill—a little farther away from my parents' house. I don't believe it: dry, dead leaves. Yet it's clearly the beginning of summer."

He tries to see a normal tree. He can't do it. His tree image can't be simply replaced with one he evaluates as positive. This is what he has to look at: the image wants to tell him something. He imagines that these trees may have died, but then he feels they're too vigorous for that, and comes up with the idea that they are in an untimely "phase of regeneration."

This makes sense to him, in the context of his life. For years, he has worked hard to get his father's business back on even keel, and has come up with new ideas for it. He has been very successful, but now—at the wrong time, he feels—he has become unable to eat. He just can't do it anymore. He needs time for regeneration.

Whether they're stopped or not, disturbing images must always be scrutinized as to the message they want to convey to us.

Ability to control, however, doesn't mean only the ability to stop negative images but quite generally the imaginer's ability to deal with interior figures, the fears released by them, the stimulation or overstimulation they may bring with them, in such a manner that the imaginative process does not come to a halt. For that reason, it is useful to memorize certain strategies for dealing with interior figures.

Strategies of Intervention

CHAPTER ELEVEN

ACTIVE IMAGININGS have the greatest transformative effect when the images are lively, include different sensory modalities, and are really experienced in an emotional sense while we retain some control over them and are even able to intervene in the process with our ego without bringing them to a standstill. The more we know how to deal with difficult situations that occur in the imagining, i.e., the more our anxiety is contained, the better we'll be able to let the interior images flow.

Thus it makes sense to learn a few strategies of intervention. In the therapeutic process, this can be done by having the analyst accompany the analysand's imagining while having the latter verbalize it continuously in such a way that the analyst is always able to suggest, within the frame of the images, how to deal with a particular situation. In time, these pointers will be internalized by the imaginer, who is then able to use them without assistance by the therapist.

Reading recorded examples of imaginings (outside therapy sessions), one may also be able to recreate these in one's own imagination and thus acquire a repertory of possibilities of conduct for difficult situations. It may well be that one then behaves quite differently from the person in the example, and there is nothing wrong with that; the important thing is the acquisition of a feeling of competence in dealing with imagined situations.

While there is an infinite number of intervention strategies, a few essential ones will be cited here, to facilitate a degree of assurance in dealing with imaginings. This gives us a relative degree of freedom from anxiety, and makes it possible to let our creative potential unfold in the imaginings.

Fairy tales provide a great number of intervention strategies. I will discuss a few that seem essential to me.[58]

Facing What Terrifies

As the fairy tale "The Purple Flower" clearly demonstrates, the monster, once seen—even if that sight causes one to faint for a moment—generates less fear in subsequent encounters. It is easier to deal with a situation once we've really taken a good look at it, instead of looking away. This fundamental idea is already contained in the suggestion: "Imagine . . . Now look closely; what does it look like?"

To take a look, to look closely, always involves no longer avoiding or repressing something or someone, but recognizing and accepting it. When we, in our imagining, look an animal in the eye, this means not only that we're trying to hold it at bay with our eyes, but also that we become fully cognizant of its existence.[59]

Finding the Interior Companion

In fairy tales of the "grateful dead" type, e.g., the Norwegian tale "The Comrade"[60] or the Kurdish tale "Red

Hair—Green Eyes,"[61] the hero is confronted with the choice of either going out into the world or taking over his father's business. On his way into the world he sees a scene in which a dead body receives a whipping. When the surprised hero asks about the reason for this, he is told that the dead man, while he was still alive, had defaulted on a debt, or had diluted wine with water, or some similar thing. The good-hearted hero decides to redeem the body, and it is given a decent burial. After a short while, the hero is joined by a mysterious companion who is able to predict problematic situations and knows how to deal with them. The hero finds that he can trust the companion implicitly. After the hero has gained enough experience and also lost his naïveté in regard to dealings with evil, the companion disappears with the explanation that he is the spirit of the redeemed dead man, which was why one could rely on him not only in questions related to life, but also in those related to death.

This interior companion, who may be male or female, complements the hero or heroine but is more involved in the complexities of life than the latter, and knows more about the secrets of life. The interior companion may also appear spontaneously in active imaginings, and in those, too, he or she often embodies an aspect one has previously redeemed, liberated, by accepting it despite its burden of guilt.

At first, these are figures—even in our sleeping dreams —we don't love, don't find agreeable, since they don't correspond to the ideal image we've made of ourselves, and hence are difficult to accept as aspects of ourselves. Often there are long imagining sequences of rapprochement to these figures, involving numerous conflicts before these aspects are accepted. If we succeed in taking these "shadow aspects" in, we have accepted an aspect of ourselves, i.e., "redeemed" it; and the ego gains additional degrees of freedom. After an interior dispute with an interior figure, that figure almost always becomes a reliable companion for a certain time in the imagining.

However, the companion may also be a known or unknown person who is important to one—with whom one often enters into a dialogue, to conduct an interior dispute in a very cordial manner, and this gives one the feeling of not being a solitary victim of life's problems. Other companions confirm the imaginer, provide her or him with security; others become idealized companions.

At the same time, these companions may also be experienced as figures which can no longer be understood simply as personality aspects but as true "guests" in one's own psyche. Such a figure may partake of the numinous: its appearance and existence are always tinged with strangeness, yet it also seems very familiar, it belongs to one while extending far beyond oneself. It then belongs to the company of companions who can't be simply managed but show up and leave whenever it suits them.

In this way, these interior companions may exist quite close to our consciousness and represent shadow aspects of ourselves. We have to accept them, and they will, by their view of things, provide new openings of certain perspectives and help us circumnavigate reefs we hadn't noticed before. But they may also involve us in difficulties we could have done without. Later, however, we find that working our way through these has been important for us.

On the other hand the interior companions may also be able to connect us with the depth of our unconscious. Behind the shadow figure may appear an interior figure of a numinous character, one that belongs—yet also does not belong—to us.

In a therapy situation, the analyst may often act as an interior companion. He or she also becomes the carrier of shadow aspects that have to be discussed and finally accepted. They may become idealized, or may idealize the analysand, but they may also become carriers of an image of an interior companion that extends far beyond their conscious personality.

Direct suggestions for imaginings may be used to find or choose an interior companion, if he or she has not already come to the fore as an agent in a dream.

Possible suggestion:
Imagine that you're going on a mysterious journey on which you have to deal with a few problems.

Whom do you choose as your companion? This should be a person you don't know.

Together with her or him, transpose yourself into a certain landscape. How does this look, what do you see, smell, hear, feel?

The mood expressed in the imagining indicates whether the imaginer feels good in the company of this interior companion.

Very frequently, it takes time and patience to recognize such an interior companion; they are not simply given to one.

Example from therapeutic work: The point of departure is a thirty-eight-year-old woman's dream:

I stand in front of a locked house, i.e., in front of a locked door. I don't know the house, but I know that I have to go in. I've rung the bell, knocked, etc. No one comes.

Then a woman approaches, with quick, resolute steps.

She seems positively tomboyish, has one of those incredibly short haircuts, but does not strike me as unsympathetic. I wake up.

The first thing that occurs to the dreamer is that the other woman's haircut was incredibly short yet not unsympathetic, a shaven head. With that woman, she thinks, she might be able to find a way into the house. The woman might even be capable of forcing her way in.

Even in the dream, a certain ambivalence toward this female figure is apparent. In the associations, this ambivalence becomes apparent again: the complicated evaluation of the hairstyle has to do with the evaluation of the figure as a whole.

Such ambivalent feelings toward a possible interior companion occur frequently. I ask the analysand to gather further impressions of the dream woman by visualizing her once more. The analysand sees her as resolute, unbridled, spontaneous to the degree of impulsive, masculine: "She does wear her hair like a man. She is a little too brash, too resolute, but she knows what she wants, and that isn't so bad per se. . . ."

Now the analysand, too, becomes aware that her feelings toward this woman are of a dual nature. She doesn't like women of this type, is even a little afraid of them, but keeps dreaming about them, and has the impression she should develop aspects of her femininity symbolized by this type. She adds that she envies the type—these women are her "opposites." She herself takes so much trouble to be accommodating, "gently feminine, so terribly feminine. . . ." Then she laughs.

The female aspects this analysand foregrounds are obvious: as a woman, she wants to be seen as gentle, feminine, etc. I don't experience her as merely gentle and accommodating but often see her as very resolute, even steely at times. She, however, doesn't yet want to recognize those aspects. But she is able to laugh about her desire to be so "terribly feminine." Then she says: "I suppose I'll have to accept that side of me, I don't think it's so bad at all, but I have to watch out that this woman doesn't walk over me. I simply need her, because I can't get into this house without her, and I have to get into the house."

It is typical that the interior companion is accepted with great reluctance and only because the imaginer knows that she does not, by herself, stand a chance of entering the house. At first, this interior companion shows herself as the dreamer's "opposite." At first: we never know what further aspects may lie hidden behind these figures. Interior companions are often opposites to our own ways of representing, showing ourselves to the world. In time, they may change to such a great degree that they strike one as brothers or sisters, very similar to oneself, with whom one goes through trials. Or else they become numinous figures.

About the house, the dreamer says she knows only that she must enter it urgently; it seems most essential for her life to go in there. From the outside, the house is quite unassuming; it's surrounded by leaves and appears green — everything is extraordinarily green and overgrown, she can smell the green, it smells like life. Inside that house one would be really secure and alive. Security is a very important theme in this woman's life. She grew up with adoptive parents but lost both of them in an accident and subsequently lived in various homes. Hence, security is important. She only feels secure in the company of other people, but even then only if she can fit in perfectly. Even in that case she does not feel entirely comfortable, because she is then no longer able to express and fulfill her own needs.

Dreams that don't achieve closure, that end with a situation one would like to change—represented here in the dreamer's conviction that she must get into that house—lend themselves well to work with the imaginative technique. It is a matter of continuing processes inspired by one's own unconscious.

I ask the analysand to imagine the final dream image once again, as vividly as possible.

She sees herself in front of the door, describes herself at length, standing in front of the door, then describes the door. "I can see myself ringing the bell, knocking, shouting, ringing the bell again. I have a familiar sense of impotence, I'm close to tears, I feel totally helpless and abandoned.

"Here comes the resolute woman. I look at her. She grins. This makes me insecure. I say to her: 'You make me feel insecure but I'm glad you're here, I need you.' She nods, doesn't say anything; she doesn't seem defensive but does not really extend herself to me. She starts working on the door, but to no avail. Then, suddenly, she says: 'Sometimes you can't get into a house because you're trying the wrong entrance. The entrance isn't always where the door is.'

"Her words amaze me. If she thinks I'll climb through a window in this tight skirt . . . I'm very reluctant, but I can't withdraw. She takes my hand. I think: There we are, now I'm just a little kid whose hand has to be held. My anger makes it so I can't sense the woman anymore. Now I get angry with myself. I can't use this anger now, I have to stop it."

I advise the analysand to breathe deeply, to relax, and then I ask her to imagine, once again, the image that triggered her anger.

"I try to feel myself next to the woman again who is holding my hand. She is back. She leads me around the house—very resolutely. She starts turning over a compost heap, hands me another shovel. I'm afraid I'll get my clothes dirty but I go along with it, thinking, I can always take them to the dry cleaners later."

Here the analysand interrupts the imagining, extremely surprised by the turn it has taken, and then says it's apparent she has to turn over her own compost a little before doing anything else. She is, however, convinced that this labor is an essential condition for her gaining access to the house. This image, as well, is worth returning to.

During the next session the analysand suggests we continue. Once again, she imagines garbage and describes it: it is no longer garbage but has turned into good soil that now needs to be turned over. She notices that she's wearing appropriate clothes this time. She continues:

"We dig, we move the entire heap. But when it seems we're done with that task, my companion goes on digging, quite fanatically, and reveals a passage into the ground. The resolute one squeezes herself into it and beckons to me to follow her. I'm afraid, it is dark. My companion doesn't seem to mind the darkness, perhaps it even doesn't seem so dark to her. After a while, I can see better: we're in a cave that seems quite cozy. And there's an old friend of mine. But I don't want to meet him, I've been wanting to forget him, he was the one who was so sadistic, always tormented me. I had really expected something beautiful down here, perhaps a circular drawing on the cave wall, a sphere. But the old friend blocks my way—he's looking for an argument. Suddenly I sense the resolute one standing behind me, very close, I can sense her body and her breath. In a whisper, she tells me how to behave. I am overcome by a very warm feeling for her, and I feel somewhat safe even in this horrible situation."

The imagining clearly shows how an ambivalent, once-experienced dream figure is first re-experienced ambivalently but can then be accepted with increasing ease. This woman, called "the resolute one" by the imaginer, takes control, knows more than the imaginer herself.

It is interesting that she can experience the desired feeling of safety to a certain degree when, in this frightening confrontation with a friend who has been experienced as a sadist, this resolute woman literally covers her back, probably fortifies it, and clearly gives her the feeling that she's not alone, that this woman is aiding her.

For the analysand, this was an overwhelming recognition. No one from outside was helping her, not even I, her therapist, but a woman from her dream, a figure she was able to imagine at any time and who did appear in her imagining, a woman who came to her aid even though she had at first rejected this woman—a figure toward whom she could have truly good and bad feelings without being repulsed.

This imagining was preceded by an analysis of some duration: it occurred in the forty-sixth analytical session. In our analytical relationship, the analysand often projected people with whom she had important but ambivalent relationships onto me, and thus provoked the rejection she had gone through with them in her life. Since I knew that this provocation was a matter of transferences of previous experiences onto me, we were able to understand her attitude and interpret it so that she, too, was able to understand herself.

Time and again I've noticed that a relational attitude transferred to the analyst will also be transferred to the interior figures.

When an interior figure appears as an interior companion, this always indicates that the imaginer is becoming more independent and increasingly able to deal with problems on her or his own. About the Active Imagination Jung says that it is, among other things, a method for gaining more independence from the analyst. That statement holds true for imagining in general as long as the analysand is truly able to stay in touch with his or her interior images.

Patterns of Relationship
Reflected by the Imaginative Process

On the other hand, an imagining with an interior companion may well depict existing relationship patterns between the analyst and the analysand and show latent transferences, wishes, and expectations that only become apparent in the imagining.

Example from Therapeutic Practice

The relationship pattern between analysand and analyst, expressed in the terms of an imagining:

A patient formerly treated for anxiety, thirty-five years old, says she feels at the moment as if she were on a difficult mountain trek, trying to blaze a trail. Because she uses this image in her description, yet seems hardly touched, emotionally, by the difficult situation, I ask her to express this trail-blazing in an imagining.

After a brief relaxation period, she sees herself in the mountains, in an unfamiliar region. The ascent is steep, beyond any hiking trails; one has to find one's own footing. "I'm walking ahead, another woman behind me—your age, your stride. Even though it's hard going, I walk fast, perhaps too fast, almost a little frantically. I'm probably not paying enough attention to where it's really possible to proceed; over and over, I start out climbing where it isn't, then have to backtrack, feel annoyed. My companion looks pensive, hangs back. She examines the cliff face for a long time and once in a while indicates, with a hand gesture, where she thinks it may be possible to go on. It seems like she is more familiar with these mountains than I am. It occurs to me she could walk ahead and find the way, and I tell her so.

"She shakes her head, says: 'It has to be your trail.'

"I plead with her: 'Please, do it for me.'

"She shakes her head emphatically but with a friendly expression.

"Defiant, I sit down on the ground.

"Now she takes the lead. I follow her, things are much easier now. But she isn't going in the direction I had imagined: to my mind, she proceeds at far too easy an angle of ascent."

In the past, this woman had always seduced her mother into "leading the way"—after her mother had probably led the way for too long in the woman's early childhood—and showing her trails that didn't frighten her. As a person with a great deal of fear, she was in the habit of finding helpers, both male and female, to solve her many problems. At first, they seemed to provide genuine relief from anxiety but then, of course, allowed the analysand to become increasingly helpless. This feeling of helplessness, and the feeling of a lack of competence in dealing with problems—combined with her early childhood experience of not really being granted autonomy and having to leave that matter to grown-ups—caused her anxiety to expand. In therapy, she had learned to take more responsibility for herself, and had thus gained autonomy. But at this moment, when it has become necessary for her to really find her own way, she tries to reinstate the old relationship patterns in her imagining.

Her companion—my age, and what's more, my "stride"—is, most likely, myself, her therapist. The analysand tends to make frantic decisions. It seems that I'm balancing that out by introducing a rather more introspective moment into the relationship. Yet, in her imagining the analysand manages to seduce me into acting as her helper and finding a way for her to proceed. Predictably, that seduction proves useless: I choose a trail that isn't steep enough for her taste. This relationship pattern, made manifest in her imagining, does not apply only to her and myself, but also to other persons and herself: over and over again, she manages to maneuver others into helping her, only to criticize them later, without fail. This criticism then mostly makes her own agenda clear to her.

Behavior in everyday life, and even behavior in therapy situations, can certainly be reflected in these imaginings which then serve as a basis for conclusions on actual relationship patterns. Very frequently the imaginer realizes, in the process of imagining, inside of which relationship patterns he or she is living, or would like to live. Even here, the question arises whether this relationship pattern really is a lived one, or whether it is a yearned-for pattern, one that possibly might lead to more satisfaction. In the case of this analysand, experiences in the therapeutic relationship, as well as descriptions of actual relationships, made it clear that her relationship pattern was an actually lived one.

Yearned-for Relationship Patterns

In addition, imagining may also reveal relationship patterns that point to the future, relationship patterns of yearning—first experienced in the imagining.

Example: A forty-five-year-old man dreams about an unknown woman he finds very fascinating. His recall of the dream is faint, he can barely imagine the woman again. What remains in the waking state is this fascination that made him feel exuberant and that he wanted to hold on to.

I ask him to concentrate on this feeling and to imagine the woman, as best he can, in surroundings that seem to correspond with the feeling. His imagining:

"I'm walking along a path I know well from my student days. It's a path across meadows, there are a couple of trees here and there, views into a valley. The sun is shining but it isn't hot, just pleasantly warm. The woman is walking beside me—I sense her more than I can see her. Uncharacteristically, I am silent, I simply don't know what to say to her, and so I don't say anything. Now, suddenly, the path runs alongside a brook, a really lively one. I sense its liveliness very intensely. I want to somehow convey this to my companion, but I don't know how to do it, I'm at a loss for words. She sits down by this brook—I can do what I want: stay or leave. But I won't leave. We both gaze at the brook. I do not even feel the need to touch my companion—which is quite contrary to my habits. I surprise myself, think: Ah, how romantic—and this breaks the imagining. I don't want to break it. I so enjoy sitting next to this woman, sensing her there; I'm not even looking at her, I don't want to impress her—we sit there looking at the brook together—we're just there."

At this point, the analysand remains silent for about five minutes. Then he detaches himself from the images and says:

"That was all there was to it—just this being there—nothing else at all. That is overwhelming. I've never been able to do that with anyone—just to be there; least of all with a woman—there I'm immediately under pressure to perform, to sell myself—we already know that, don't we. Just to be."

The analysand had the impression that it was the woman, this mysterious stranger whom he was not supposed to scrutinize too closely, who brought about his behavior in the imagining. She vivified the side of him that only wants to "be," to enjoy what it encounters: that joy appears in the shape of the lively brook. Yet he didn't feel dominated by her but sensed himself free to stay and free to leave.

This relationship pattern was new to him, and it was new to me, as well, in my relationship with him. He also knew that it was this kind of relationship he was really yearning for, one in which he could feel wordlessly but deeply connected to someone.[62] But he also knew that this kind of relationship, with its attendant feelings, was at that time only attainable in the imagination.

The interior companion, male or female, is often related to people who actually accompany us in some form in our everyday life. They are sometimes seen in the shape of our lovers or spouses, sometimes as their opposites. If imaginings with interior companions are pursued over an extended period, it will be experienced that they have other qualities than those we perceive in actual fellow humans. Interior companions revive feelings in us with which we are not familiar and hence cause behavior that is new to us, even in our behavior towards other people.

The need for such an interior companion in the imagining arises when interior paths are new paths, frightening ones, or ones that proceed into the depths; it also arises when imaginers want to share their experiences and want to find themselves in another person.

Recognizing the Wise Old Man or Woman

Fairy tales often begin with the absence of something essential—say, the water of life,[63] or the golden apples disappear in an inexplicable way,[64] or a child is not born.[65] Princes, princesses, kings, or queens then set forth to seek what is so painfully missing, the way we too set forth at times because we can no longer endure a lack and want to have new experiences in order to bring something new into our lives.

Yet there are times when it's very hard to know where to look and what to look for. The fairy-tale heroes and heroines have just as hard a time of it. Once they've decided to take the risk and to simply set forth into the world without any guarantee they'll find what they're looking for, they encounter, mostly at the edge of a forest—i.e., where normal possibilities of orientation cease—an old man or an old woman. He or she may also be encountered by the shore of some sea; they are always met where, for the searcher, a "new world" begins, and where it is important to find the right way. These old men and women are frequently in rags, or they may appear in the shape of talking animals.[66]

If heroine or hero sit down by the forest's edge to have something to eat, to fortify themselves for the road, these old people often join them and ask them to share. If the victuals are not shared and no answers are given to questions about "whence" and "where to," one may be certain that this particular hero or heroine will soon be detained somewhere—either stuck between boulders[67] or at the noisy wayside inn, forgetful of their original intent to bring back home something of vital importance.

But if the searchers acknowledge this old woman or man, even share their food with her or him, and then tell him or her why they are looking for something, then they are assured of his or her assistance, even if the advice given may at first sound a little strange.

These advisers are always old, unsightly, sometimes of animal form. They beg, i.e., ask to be considered. Who customarily only sees the exterior does not regard them worthy of a reply and disdains their advice. Who is more intent on his or her search, mostly even worried because it is so unclear how this often unknown necessity of life is to be obtained, who is afraid or has already exhausted all conscious possibilities and is in genuine despair because no solution is in sight, is delighted with any advice, is no longer preoccupied with superficialities, is ready to share what bread is left, and the story of his or her own misfortune, with anyone willing to do so.

These old men and women always ask one to consider: Whence do you come? What are you searching for?

Then they give advice—because they know where the water of life can be found, or which herbs will help the queen become pregnant at last. However, the heroes and heroines have to undertake the search by themselves: only rarely does the old person accompany them, perhaps in the shape of an animal.

It is also typical for these fairy tales that the wise old man or woman points out the dangers that threaten if his or her advice isn't followed to the letter. Heroines and heroes never quite manage to do so, and thus they acquire further problems at first, but end up experiencing more, and mostly gaining more than they initially intended. The advice of the wise old man or woman is very important, but it seems to be equally important that while one starts out following the advice as to the right direction, one then pursues one's own intentions and wishes—thus doesn't just do what the old person has told one to do but puts one's own stamp on the search.

When we're engaged in a quest in our imagination, and our conscious ego no longer knows what to do next, when we're perhaps despairing a little, it may be useful to remember that advice from a wise old woman or man could come in handy now. If we know these figures from dreams, or if we have met a wise old person in literature who caught our fancy, we'll try to revive that figure in our imagination.

The best way to tell that it really is a wise old person is to see if he or she will give us advice that seems nonsensical at first. If these wise old people tell us what we already know, or what authority figures have been telling us all our lives, it's quite possible they are not of the kind that is familiar with the larger conscious and unconscious contexts of life, but merely old familiar interior voices perhaps derived from fathers, grandfathers, or teachers. These, too, may be wise but are not necessarily so. True wise old persons are unknown and yet familiar—and they fascinate us.

Possible instruction for imagining:
You have a difficult task ahead of you. You have an inkling but don't really know what it is you must find. You set out on a journey—you know for certain that that is what you must do.

You reach the edge of a forest and see a figure sitting there—an old man, an old woman. (If you see someone else or an animal there, follow your imagination.)

This figure asks you for food and wants to know whence you come and where you are going. Answer to the best of your ability and wait for advice.

Wise old persons are also seen against a background of memories of mothers, grandmothers, fathers, and grandfathers.

When we turn to a wise old person, this may be an indication of our emergence from a mother or father complex. *Behind* mothers and fathers we can now recognize the archetype of the wise old person, i.e., we can consider and accept a wisdom that has nothing to do with the struggle for autonomy and the separation problems we experience with concrete parents, or the boundary definition problems we have because we resemble our parents yet must become entirely individual persons, ourselves. As long as these wise old persons tell us what we could tell ourselves, or what father and mother have always told us, they're still mostly personifications of our mother and father complexes. Even that may be very useful in a therapeutic context, as an engagement between the ego complex and the parent complex, of the kind that proves necessary once in a while to enable the ego to truly differentiate itself from the parents—in other words, become an adult. This is not to say that one has to become different from one's parents at any cost, that one has to embrace opinions that differ from theirs no matter what, simply in order to appear separate and grown up, but we do have to decide which of our parents' types of behavior, opinions, ideas truly belong to us and agree with us so that we really want to represent them, and which ones don't.

It is, however, necessary to be close observers of our imagination. If we retain paternal or maternal maxims in our psyches as advice given by wise old persons, we block access to the true wise old persons, access that may not be really available at that particular moment but could be kept open as a path of yearning.

This expectation of an encounter with the figure of a wise old person may also lead us to an emergence out of a captivity in a father and mother complex.

Example from therapeutic work: I want to present the imagining of a fifty-four-year-old man who suffers from severe depressive episodes, has a fundamental tendency to blame himself a great deal, and makes a rather self-tormented impression.

The starting point consisted of a dream image: a fish he'd been holding wriggled out of his hand, fell down a sewer hole—and disappeared. The dream triggered great sadness in him.

The analysand has been trained in the imaginative technique and expresses the wish to follow his fish in his imagination. His imagining:

I find myself in a sewer tunnel, below the street, looking for my fish. The place is horribly dirty. I'm really seeing images from a film—a movie set in the underground sewer system of the city of Paris, I think it was a thriller, the sewers were used as escape routes. I look around, there are rats flitting everywhere, the stench is incredible. What possessed me to come here! There are a great number of branching tunnels down there, it is confusing. As time goes by, I begin to feel frightened, I sense my heart beating so much faster that I have trouble breathing—but this may also be due to the stench. It seems possible that I won't find the fish but also that I won't find my way out back to the surface again. My breath gets very short.

The analysand manifests all the symptoms of fear, and I tell him: "You need help. Breathe out deeply, a couple of times." He does so, calms down a little, then says:

My father (who was a miner) appears, with a miner's lantern. I worry about the old man: he might slip and fall. I'm ashamed because I called him to come and help me, and annoyed because I chose to call him. He is mumbling to himself, I can hardly hear it, but what he seems to be saying is: You always were foolhardy, well, who can afford to just lose fish like that, my miserable son, who can afford to lose fish. All my bitterness rises in me: always recriminations, never help, even when I could use it. Except for this little bit of light from the lantern—but I don't even need that. (He takes another deep breath.)

I thank my father and show him a way out through a shaft directly above us. He leaves, hands me the lantern before he does. I'm grateful for that, and walk on at a quick pace.

He then goes on to talk about the smell, the dirt, how slippery it is. . . . He tries to remember if the actors in the film weren't roped up, but can't be sure; it occurs to him that being roped up requires a second person.

After a long while he meets a bum. He thinks that this man must know his way about the sewers. He approaches the bum and hands him a small bottle of schnapps.

Bum: *What do you want?*

Imaginer: *I'm looking for my fish.*

B.: *What do you want to do with it?*

I.: *I want to see where it takes me.*

B.: *So you'll follow it?*

I.: *Yes, but I'm at my wit's end.*

B.: *Do you have any more schnapps?*

(The imaginer hands him another small bottle.)

B.: *Sit down with me.*

I.: *The stench is killing me.*

B.: *You get used to it.* (Proffers the schnapps bottle.)

I.: (Drinks, impatiently.)

At some point, the bum mumbles: *"You have to go back to the place where you parted from your father, and then a little farther back, that's where the clog is. Take care of the clog."*

I think that this is just a bunch of nonsense but I do go back, I find the way to the place where I sent my father off—it really is easier with this miner's lantern—and then I proceed even farther back, to a narrow passage with a round opening: this opening is clogged up with feces and dirt.

Now I have found the clog, but how will I get rid of it? I stop to ponder: did the old guy say anything about that? Then it makes me furious that he hasn't said anything, that he's told me only half the truth. Am I supposed to touch that clog? No!

Suddenly two workmen appear with high-pressure hoses. They say: "You can't really mess around with that, you just have to turn up the pressure full blast." The clog is blown away and all of us walk away, very quickly, and climb back up through a shaft.

Now I'm back in the fresh air and light—it's an incredible relief, it's like being born again.

Later the analysand says he hadn't been thinking about the fish anymore but had merely enjoyed this feeling of freedom, of being in the light and air.

This imagining shows quite clearly how the father can be separated from a figure who belongs more to the motif realm of the wise old man.

The analysand's father reproaches (and has reproached) him with the things of which he also accuses him in the imagining. The father is also jealous of his comparative affluence, but is on the other hand proud of a son who has risen higher in the world than himself. He will, however, never tell his son this. To the son, he shows his disapproval, calling him scum and accusing him of getting embroiled in all kinds of crap.

An aspect of the clog, and also the reason why the father appeared, becomes clear: the analysand can't let go of these paternal value judgments that partly stem from his childhood but have also been repeated later. He remains stuck with the negative self-image prescribed by his father, even though he knows that it is not the whole truth.

Thus, the father is finally unable to be of any help here, although he does give the son his lantern. But only the bum knows how to proceed from here.

The solution is simple: the clog has to be dealt with by means of high pressure, of concentrated energy. The bum behaves in a manner comparable to that of wise old persons in fairy tales—yet has his own character in being a drunkard. On the other hand, he demands consideration, gives a piece of advice, but does not describe in detail what the imaginer will have to do.

He does, however, point out the importance of going past the place where the imaginer left his father, i.e., to go beyond it, and yet to be very aware of that spot as a point of orientation. The bum also points out to him that he has already left his father.

What about the fish, the initial object of the search? Fish live in water and share many of its characteristics while being tangible. Hence they are considered symbols of unconcious content, they carry something from the unconscious to the conscious but are slippery, hard to grasp, unable to speak our language. They can also be seen as sexual symbols;[68] the entire sewer sequence may also be seen as an encounter with a very subterranean form of sexuality, with fears of dirt, etc.

The bum is, of course, not merely the personification of an old sage, he is also a bum who through his existence expresses the fact that he wants to be marginalized; in this figure, the imaginer meets his own "bum" aspect which he has denied so far.

Yet a wise old man is also speaking to him through this man's mouth, and he experiences a sense of freedom as he admits to having and living such bum aspects.

Wise old women and men rarely allow their wisdom to be outwardly recognizable. If one wishes for their advice, one has to be wise enough oneself to be able to recognize a wise old person.

On Dealing with Animals in the Imagining

Animals often appear in the imagining. They are close to us in everyday life, either as pets who may also be our companions, or as affectionate nicknames for fellow humans. We may find, for instance, that we've behaved "like jackasses," we say that someone is "proud as a peacock," etc. It almost seems easier to imagine our family (or another group) as animals and to depict them as such in drawings, rather than in their human form, and it is usually quite easy to find out which animal represents which person, whether we're actually drawing or just imagining these creatures.

What impresses us about individuals often immediately strikes us when we project it onto an animal. This has to do with the fact that we are close to animals and know many of them, yet, on the other hand, have just enough distance from them to enable us to speak much less guardedly about people when we transpose their images into those of animals: it makes it possible to say something about fellow humans without speaking about them directly.

When, for instance, we find ourselves in a conflict in a relationship, we may be able to see our situation and the relationship better if we imagine ourselves and our spouse or lover as animals in certain situations. Thus, a young man in a difficult relationship may say he feels like a guinea pig facing a snake, totally hypnotized. This image makes it clear that he is in great danger of being devoured unless he manages to "distract" the snake. As the image occurs to him, he does manage to come up with a distraction maneuver: he expresses surprise at the image, even finds it appalling, then gains distance and says: ". . . 'snake' is a little exaggerated—maybe more like cat and dog . . ." now seeing himself as a cat, his girlfriend as a dog.

This girlfriend, whom her boyfriend has first seen as a snake, sees the two of them as two snails that would like to hide themselves in one another totally but are constantly hampered by their own shells.

Such images make it possible to draw conclusions about fantasies regarding the relationship[69] as well as fears, aggressions, and projections. The medium of animal imagining allows for many degrees of freedom and is less frightening than a situation in which we would have to tell a partner directly what our feelings are. Very often only such an image can clarify how we experience the relationship emotionally and in a mood-related sense.

It is obvious that in the case of the above-mentioned couple the relational dynamics are very different at the moment of conflict—and such images represent the present, usually conflict-laden situation—from those between a different couple where he sees the situation as two fighting mountain goats and she sees two wildcats hissing at each other, then striking out with their paws. Both members of the latter couple assume identical species, and the possibility of fighting back.

In most cases, we are still quite in touch with our animal aspect; we know what we mean when we call ourselves "vain as a peacock," "dumb as an ox," "sly as a fox," or say we're "hungry as a wolf," etc.

Hence, animals put in frequent appearances in our imagination, as helpful animals, perhaps even animal companions, or as threatening creatures that may cause us to feel fear and panic. In order to deal with frightening animals we need to learn a few strategies with the objective of turning them, if at all possible, into helpful, friendly companions, aiding us with their special capabilities, both in the imagination and in everyday life.

Imaginings in which animals appear mostly start out with a conflict, and this corresponds to our experience that we have a great many conflicts with our "animal" aspects: problems concerning body and soul, or body and spirit, always play a part in human lives. To put it more concretely: we realize that we're still quite able to deal with, say, our fox-like aspects, but what about the swine in us, or our serpentine aspect? Acceptance of an animal aspect will of course vary according to our life stories; who loves cats will experience her or his own feline aspects as downright charming, whereas others may find cats and feline aspects deplorable, even frightening.

Our physicality, our urges and instincts, represent themselves by animal symbols, always expressing in them the wisdom inherent in our bodies.

Imaginings in which animals occur are often very lively and active; they have to do with our energy and vitality, and their effect is invigorating. Yet, while these imaginings revive us, they may also produce a great deal of fear. Conflicts between animals may be imagined, or conflicts between animals and the imaginer.

These animals may represent real blockages, but if one is able to deal with them, the experience of being blocked may open up new possibilities for one's life.

Animals must be perceived, looked at, and accepted. Animals that are ignored in our imaginations mostly react quite aggressively—just as urges we suppress or divert may manifest themselves in unpleasant ways. But if they are perceived, one will be able to let them co-exist in a modified form, if need be.

Time and again, fairy tales remind us that we shouldn't kill animals. If we let them live, they often become animal companions, even capable of saving our lives in decisive moments, as for instance in Grimms' "The Two Brothers."[70] After the two brothers have been taught how to hunt, one of them sets forth into the world. When he finds himself at his wit's end with hunger, he decides to shoot an animal, but every animal he wants to shoot tells him: "Dear hunter, let me live, I'll give you two of my young." Thus, the young hunter proceeds through the world with a whole caravan of animal companions who help him to get food for himself as well as them. Because he hasn't hastily resorted to killing, and has been able to endure hunger for quite a long time, he gets to know all these animals, all the animal aspects of himself. The animals first help him in his fight with the dragon who demands an annual sacrifice of a virgin and thus threatens the entire country with ultimate extinction. When, exhausted after the battle, he falls asleep after telling his animals to keep watch, the equally exhausted creatures also fall asleep; but when they wake up and see that the hunter has been decapitated, the hare is sent out to bring back the herb of life, and the animals' intervention revives him.

If the heroine or hero spares animals' lives and lets them live along with him or herself, they, in turn, help the hero or heroine to achieve a better life.[71] In other words: When we allow our physical aspects, urges, and instincts to live with us, when we accept our physicality and perceive what it tells us about ourselves, and thus accept physical pointers as to how we could change our way of life, this enables us to lead a better life.

Threatening Animals

Even if, at times, a fairy tale monster may be redeemed by a timely kiss, we mustn't assume that this attempt at rapprochement leads to success in each and every case. Animals may seem very threatening to us, and thus evoke a real sense of danger. Naïveté is not appropriate in dealings with these powers: careful attention has to be paid to the way these animals express themselves, before we can decide how to deal with them.

Helping: In fairy tales, animals sometimes require help: there may be a thorn stuck in a paw, a bullet lodged in a leg, even a bee buzzing in an ear.[72] These animals, driven by pain to act more or less aggressively, may be pacified by removing the cause for that pain. The animals the hero or heroine has thus helped promise to return the favor when necessary. This helpful attitude goes beyond mere acceptance. It makes it clear to the human being that he or she causes or has caused pain to his or her animal aspects—and he or she then strives to remove and to avoid the causes of such pain. In addition, such help also includes taking care that the animals may live in their proper element, fish in water, for example. In this way, one ensures the continuity of a natural order.

This does not always apply when the animals have the gift of speech. Fairy tales often feature talking animals, in other words, animals that wish to establish contact with human beings, possibly human beings who have been transformed into animals by evil spells.[73] When animals talk, they are almost human, and like fairy-tale princes and princesses that have been changed into animals which are also capable of speech, they represent aspects of ourselves we have repressed and can't accept as wholly or only partially human. The image choice also reflects a collective value judgment, according to which the animal isn't only different from the human being but also isn't worth as much. If it were perceived simply as a creature of a different nature, we could deal with it more easily.

Animals that speak want to communicate with us, show their anthropomorphic aspect; they want to and can be understood. One has to talk to them and listen to what they have to say. In imaginings, animals don't speak all that often; only sometimes, due to the impressions fairy tales have made on us, does it seem to us that they ought to be able to talk. Yet sometimes it seems more important to observe the animals' behavior closely and establish contact with them in that way, e.g., by observing their movements and then asking ourselves when it is that we move, have moved, or would like to move in similar ways.

Even when they don't speak, animals often point out the way in our imaginings, by the paths they themselves follow, and by the behavior they demonstrate.

Establishing Contact: Whether the contact established is loving or not so loving, it is in any case quite essential. In the fairy tale about the Frog King,[74] the frog is thrown against the wall, and this causes him to metamorphose into a dazzlingly handsome prince. It's not at all certain that a kiss from the princess would have effected the same transformation. We'll never know. But the example shows us that it is essential to establish contact; if a hero or heroine is terrified by the animal, this contact may take less caring forms.

This necessity of contact may also be transferred to the imagining. To perceive animals, to refrain from killing them, to help them when necessary, to take care that they can return to their own element if, somehow, they have been taken out of it; to speak to them, to engage in conversation with them and thus to try to find out if the spell that affects them can be broken; in each and every case, to establish some form of contact with them—these are the essential strategies for dealing with animals. If none of these work, or if the animals take a hostile attitude toward one, we may, as a last resort, try to feed them.

Feeding: In the fairy tale "The Water of Life,"[75] two lions guard the gate of the castle protecting the well of the water of life. The wise old man who has told the boy how to find his way to this well of life has also suggested that he take two little loaves of bread along in order to pacify the guard lions.

When we feed animals, we give away something of ours, to indicate that we are ready to empathize with their needs—thus, our own animal aspects—and ready to satisfy them. By acting this way we also demonstrate that we are able to establish a connection between aggression/ destruction and hunger: if we let aspects of ourselves go hungry, they may express themselves destructively.

Dealing with animals in our imagining is an ambivalent business. On one hand, we really have to establish contact with them; on the other, it is quite possible that an encounter with them frightens us to such a degree that we have to run away or seek out a companion who knows further strategies, or bring on other animals with whom we've already made friends, in order to be able to deal with these wild ones—with these hardly accessible aspects of ourselves that are nonetheless alive at this moment.

It is no accident that there are, and have to be, so many strategies for dealing with animals. Animals are very close to us, they're always present where there are people, yet they also remain somewhat alien. In imaginings outside the therapeutic framework we often detach ourselves from images in which frightening animals appear. After considering possible strategies we may recall the frightening image and then deal with this particular animal. It may also be helpful to consider the significance of this particular animal aspect of ourselves, consider which experiential realm it may be associated with; by pondering the experience of our Active Imagination, we may achieve a transformed attitude toward that aspect.

Identification with an Animal

Jung proceeds from the premise that every figure appearing in our dreams may also represent an aspect of our own psyche, embody a side of ourselves. The form of interpretation based on this premise is called interpretation on the subjective level—as opposed to interpretation on the objective level, in which people who occur in dreams are related to existing persons. According to the idea of the subjective level, everything or everyone we may meet in the exterior world also contains aspects of ourselves. What of the "outside" is important to us, is also important to us "inside," in our own psyche. Hence Jung is able to say that the process of individuation is simultaneously a subjective process of integration and an objective process in the realm of relationships.[76] Identification with a figure during Active Imagination takes the notion of the subjective level extremely seriously: for a moment, we forget the ego's point of view and transpose ourselves into the skin of another person or an animal whom we encounter in the imagining. Such identification makes these figures very real to the imaginer. There is little risk of not finding one's way back to the ego's point of view: as soon as we open our eyes, move, or yawn, we find our way back but are still able to remember quite vividly how it felt to be a particular animal.

Imaginings in which we identify with a figure should be described or drawn with particular care, since on the one hand we perceive in them the experience of identification and all the emotions connected with it and on the other are also able to see ourselves from the distance provided by the creativity of our ego-consciousness. Interior figure and ego-consciousness can then enter into a very productive dialogue.

Identification with interior figures is an important prerequisite for the technique of Active Imagination. Both the ability to identify, and the ability detach oneself again, are of great importance here.

Possible suggestion for imagining:
Imagine a landscape. Contemplate it calmly—what does it look like? Can you recognize a particular fragrance, can you hear something?

How do you feel in this landscape?

From somewhere, an animal/animals appear(s).

Establish contact, in the manner appropriate to yourself— take your time.

Detach yourself from these images, but don't open your eyes yet.

Relax, once again.

Breathe out deeply, once again.

Release tension with your breath.

Now imagine one of the images that make you feel good, a

relaxation image.
  Take your time.
  Now imagine that you yourself are an animal.
  Observe where you now are, as an animal.
  Are there other animals in those surroundings?
  Resume your human form, open your eyes, breathe out
deeply, yawn, stretch.

Imaginings with animals are very close to us and have
an inherent tendency to liveliness, which is why they
always animate us. Here, in closer detail, is an example in
which I stimulated such an identification with a figure in
the imagining.

Example from Therapeutic Practice: The starting point for
the imagining, in the twenty-first therapy session, is a
dream fragment dreamed by a thirty-six-year-old woman.
One of her greatest problems is that she does not know
what she wants. She always does what is expected from
her; she has always done what was expected from her,
what "one" does. She says she does not really know herself. Just recently, she has had her second experience of
being abandoned by a man after a relationship of many
years. From her first marriage she has twins, now seven-
teen years old. The dream fragment:
  A cat sits on my grandmother's stove, glaring at me. I am
very frightened. I wake up.
  She starts out by talking about the dream which has left
her with a feeling of both security and fear: security
because it reminded her of her grandmother's kitchen. In
the dream, it had been just like at Grandmother's house,
where she'd always liked to go to cook and bake things
with her in the cozy kitchen. On the other hand, Grandmother's place had always been a mess, things were anything but tidy. There had been times when she had been
repelled by this. Grandmother also had such a lot of

animals, chickens sitting on the stove—and many cats. As a child, she'd been terribly afraid of cats. Even now she was not too partial to them. Perhaps the fear in the dream came from the cat—but surely it was out of proportion to be so afraid of a cat? The cat had frightened her, lying there with its glittering eyes.

I suggest to the analysand that she work on this dream fragment with her imagination.

Excursus: Imaginative Work on Dreams

I consider it productive to revive dream images by imagining, and, in the case of fragmentary dreams, to extend the individual images by means of the imagining. When we work on dreams in this manner, we usually find it easy to get in touch with the emotional content of the dream.

Motifs arising from dreams, recent ones or ones we've remembered and are preoccupied by, really have something to do with our present psychic process, genuinely concern us.

There are two ways to proceed: one may concentrate on a dream image that is particularly interesting, very mysterious, or unclear. One can also re-imagine the dream, scene by scene. It is of course possible that the dream acquires other nuances in this process than those it had after the dream was written down. Inevitably, the dream content appears in an additional revision—the first revision having been made when the dream was remembered and recorded. It cannot be assumed that the retranslation into image language simply reproduces the "original" dream.

Imagining along the lines of a dream is one way of working with it; other ways consist of drawing the dream, rendering the dream with psycho-dramatic techniques, and interpreting it.

It seems to me that working with the imagination is a kind of dreamwork that stays very close to the emotions and does not preclude other kinds of working with the dream. Once a dream has been re-imagined, it is mostly possible to give it a more comprehensive interpretation than when simply gathering associations to individual images. On the other hand, even this collecting of notions related to the dream, as is common in dream interpretation, may proceed either abstractly or in a very imagistic fashion.

After relaxation I ask the analysand to imagine her grandmother's kitchen as vividly as possible. She describes the kitchen:

"It is a dark room, large, a stove in one corner, not an electric but an old-fashioned wood-burning one. There is a smell of wood, or maybe just smoke—just like at Grandmother's. The smoke irritates my eyes. The milk has boiled over. Grandmother hurries to the stove because of the milk, stumbles over a hen . . . it had a name. . . ." (She tries to remember the name. Suddenly:) "The curtains are red and white gingham. The hen's name has to be Alma. . . . Now I can't think of anything else."

The analysand starts stretching, wants to detach herself from the images. It is my impression that this imagining isn't finished, Grandmother almost stumbled over that hen, and so did the analysand, being unable to recall the name that seemed so important to her. So I ask her if it's possible for her to concentrate on the hen.

The analysand: "It cackles quite awfully and scratches the floor. It goes to the stove, it goes where the cat was lying in my dream." Extended silence.

I ask: "What does the cat look like now?"

She: "I don't see the cat in the dream but one of Grandmother's cats. It is awfully big, it's arching its back."

I ask her: "How big are you there?"

She: "I'm hardly bigger than the cat, the cat seems to be bigger than me, I'm maybe five years old. I look around for Grandmother, I want to run to her. Now she is no longer sitting there. I'm quite agitated, the cat arches its back ever higher, and Grandmother isn't there anymore. I can't run away."

The analysand pauses again, and I don't hesitate to intervene because it seems to me that she's in a state of fearful agitation: "Look at the cat, look at its eyes."

She: "It has such wild eyes, it's about to pounce on me."

My intervention hasn't diminished her fear. I ask: "Is there a milk bowl anywhere nearby?" This might be a time when feeding could help.

The analysand: "There is, I put it in front of the cat, it's lapping the milk, it seems calm now. I walk outside, thinking, well, that was a close call. I don't know why cats are so antagonistic to me."

I ask her if the opposite couldn't be true—that she has something against cats. She denies it vehemently.

"Now I go back into the kitchen, and I see the cat from the dream on the stove. Nothing moves, it doesn't move, only its eyes move, it doesn't let me out of its sight. Nothing I can do about that."

The analysand falls silent again. I still find the situation incomplete and intervene again: "It is still lying there as if it wanted to tell you something. What would it tell you if it could speak?"

"It would say"—a response at lightning speed—"'This spot on the stove belongs to me, I won't have this spot taken away from me, least of all by you. It is nice and warm here, I feel good here, just you try to chase me off!'

"I feel helpless. I want to chase it off the stove. It's unsanitary to have it lying there. But I also want to chase it away so I can get closer to the stove myself.

"I walk away, quite sad. Then it occurs to me: maybe that trick with the milk could work? I pour milk for the cat, very noisily. The cat blinks with one eye, closing the other; it seems unsure or doesn't want to make a move, but then it jumps down to the floor, stretches, and pretends it didn't leave its warm spot just because of the milk, but starts lapping it up. I'll go to Grandmother and tell her that I've tamed the wild cat."

She laughs, opens her eyes, and stretches.

In imaginings, one needs to decide not only when to intervene as a therapist, but also when to bring the imagining to a close again. When imaginers spontaneously stop imagining, this may well be the right time to conclude things for the time being, but it may also be that the imaginers are experiencing a juncture in their imagining that is particularly problematic, releases strong emotions, perhaps even reveals a key locus of which they're afraid.

The analysand may stop here because she feels that she has for the first time stood her ground in a conflict with this cat. She feels the need to tell her grandmother about her success. She has the experience of having achieved a certain degree of competence in her dealings with this particular feline.

Notions about the imagining: The analysand says that her grandmother had always been very sad because she, the analysand, was so afraid of the animals her grandmother had so enjoyed keeping around her.

"I think my objections to their unsanitary nature—which I voiced as quite a small girl—struck her as rather unbalanced. My sister was much less of a problem that way, she herself was, in fact, much like a kitten, so cuddly and affectionate, she really knew how to express her feeling of well-being. And she always took my place in Grandmother's house. She might have said: 'This place belongs to me, I won't let anyone take it away from me.'"

With this memory, the imagining connects with her childhood history. Suddenly, the sister appears as the cuddly cat that usurps her good spot at Grandmother's. All she's left with is that hissing, sharp-clawed cat. The sister was good, she herself was naughty, but only when they were at their grandmother's, where it would have been particularly important to her to be a favored grandchild.

This problem had not been brought up while we discussed her life history. Her fear of cats may have been reinforced by the undue force with which she handled them—and which, in turn, led to her being scratched now and again. On the other hand, it may also have had something to do with her fear of her sister, perhaps even a great rage against that sister, which she didn't dare express because she was dependent on her sister's assistance.

If we consider the cat in a larger symbolic context and note that this woman has a grandmother who has close relationships with animals in general and cats in particular, who relates to the animal world extremely well and could be seen as a terrestrial image of a mistress of animals,[77] a mother goddess, particularly skilled in her dealings with animals—then the analysand's fear of cats might mean that she has had, from childhood on, a fear of an instinctual femininity, one that involves living the seductive, feline aspects of the female, at least in a rudimentary sense, as her sister was able to. Once this topic is addressed in dream and imagining, it is no longer a question of a memory of security in Grandmother's kitchen and the attendant feeling of revulsion, nor is it only a question of rivalry with her sister who usurped the best spot next to Grandmother. This topic has to do with individuation, with her relationship with her feminine, feline aspect, which is related to physicality, tenderness, and also a strong striving for autonomy. All these levels have to be considered.

Even though active imaginings affect our feelings by their wealth of imagery, give us a sense of competence in dealing with the topics addressed, help us get in touch with the emotions concerned, and thus give us energy to tackle certain problems, it is still very necessary to gather associations and notions regarding these imaginings, in order to connect them with the subject's life history and to examine them with a view to their implications for the future.

Beyond giving an example of imagining that contains animals, I also wanted to point out the technique of intervention and to show that even when interventions are made out of a feel for the psychic process, they may sometimes be erroneous and may have to be replaced by further strategies.

This example also shows that interventions made by the therapist are quickly internalized, learned, and used, even in the same imagining, as when the analysand tells herself she just might try the trick with the milk again. This strikes me as the main purpose of interventions in general—to help people who tend to get stuck in the flow of their interior images, and might become discouraged from working this way, learn how to deal with difficult situations in their imaginings.

A later imagining by the same analysand (seventy-third session) demonstrates that she has assimilated the strategies of intervention. The starting point is, once again, a dream:

I'm in my kitchen. A wildcat hisses, charges about, knocks dishes off the shelves. I'm very afraid it'll get the newly hatched chickens, that it will bite them to death. I don't know whether I should try to protect the chickens or try to calm down the cat.

I wake up, frightened but angry as well: once again I haven't been able to finish a dream.

She has decided to finish this dream with active imagining. After she has relaxed, I ask her to re-imagine the dream images. She waxes rhapsodic about the soft, tender chickens:

"They arouse very tender, nurturing feelings in me. One has to deal very tenderly with these chickens. But there is this wild beast. Full of energy, aggressive, in a rage, probably because of the chickens. It is a very large red cat with glittering eyes, as always. I'm not as frightened as I used to be but I don't quite know how to deal with it. I want to look at the cat, fix it with my eyes, but it keeps dashing about. Milk seems to be the only trick left, I get the bowl. The cat calms down a little but looks at me with great suspicion while it sidles up to the bowl. But now there is a chicken at the bowl. My heart almost stops. I hurry over and put the chicken in my pocket. The cat hisses at me, enraged. I want to stroke it but know I can't do that—it would scratch me, perhaps even scratch my eyes out. Now I remember liver—liver! I get some liver out of the refrigerator. Now, at last, this mad cat is pacified and calm. I collect the chickens without letting the cat out of my sight. I'll have to tame it. For just a moment I put the chickens in the refrigerator."

To her mind, the imagining has been completed. It is, of course, questionable whether a problem has reached a provisional conclusion here; whether it has been restated in such a way that it can be worked on in a further imaginative sequence; or whether a conflict situation has been avoided.

I consider the problem defused for the time being and am able to accept her decision to stop the sequence at this point.

Clearly, the analysand has now mastered the strategies of dealing with animals and has even developed new ideas. The choice of liver is very significant: the analysand is hardly able to touch liver, due to her strong revulsion against the "bloody slippery stuff." She tells me later that she had to overcome this revulsion even in her imagining and describes in detail her horror of touching liver.

In addition, both dream and imagining show that the cat and the chickens which previously belonged to grandmother's domain have now moved close to her, into her own kitchen. She still has difficulties with the wildcat, and the cat, in turn, challenges her to touch liver, to deal with feelings she has previously found abhorrent, but also to deal quite concretely with things that she considers only too human. The ancients regarded the liver as the site of life; only when she's able to reach out and touch life in the raw will the wildcat be able to live inside her in a way appropriate to its nature.

Concluding an Imagining

It is not imperative to keep intervening, to keep the imagining going up to the point where a problem is truly solved. In my experience, a clear exposure of the problem, with a vivid experience of the individual images, is a quite satisfactory result, as it allows conflicting aspects of an imagining to unfold to their full extent.

If images really become so vivid and compelling to us that we feel we can no longer endure the emotions connected with them, should we decide to terminate the imagining and continue it on the following day? Sometimes we're surprised to find that the appropriate emotion can no longer be recaptured the next day. There are interior processes that ripen at a specific time, no sooner, no later. If we miss that moment, we really have missed something.

It may, however, be sensible to turn away from the interior images because the pertinent emotion is getting to be too much for us. It is a matter of one's own self-knowledge as a therapist to decide whether or not to intervene at such a moment in order to prevent the interior images from breaking off, or whether to guide the imaginer away from his or her images.

When active imagining is exercised in a therapeutic situation, the therapist will sense which energies are connected with the images and also know how much fear they can trigger.

If a therapist concludes an imagining before the imaginer feels it's right to end it, the latter usually objects, and the topic of not feeling understood will have to be addressed. In such a case one can concentrate on the last remembered image and wait for the interior images to start changing again.

On Dealing with the Threatening

In our imaginings we aren't threatened only by animals but also by human beings, perhaps very large or incomparably stronger than we consider ourselves to be. Sometimes we're even threatened by figures we're unable to recognize clearly, as when they are shrouded.

Various Possibilities

To recognize the threatening: When dealing with what threatens us in our imagining it is first of all, and once again, important to recognize what it is that frightens us, to take a close look, and to admit our fear. One admits to one's fear of what one experiences as a threat, then lets this threatening material, often sensed to be "evil," exist alongside of oneself. It's the purpose of fear to make us aware of threats and alert us to find ways and take steps to alleviate the situation.

Although it is essential to develop one's courage to be afraid (Jaspers)—if we don't, we won't confront the world enough—it is also important, in the practice of active imagination, to discover the point up to which we're able to deal with our fear and past which we can no longer do so. In order to achieve this, we have to find out what the situations are in which we react with fear.

To address the aspect that inspires confidence: This presupposes the assumption that a figure is not totally evil, but that it is the image evoked by our fear which lets such a figure appear to be so.

In fairy tales, the turn toward a confidence-inspiring aspect takes the form of the hero's dealing with the devil's grandmother instead of the devil himself, whom he was originally told to visit,[78] or, in the case of another hero, his addressing Baba Yaga (who is sharpening her teeth to devour him) as "little mother" and thus awakening her gentler, more maternal feelings. Instead of making a meal of him, she cooks one for the hero and gives him a crucial piece of advice.[79] This strategy points out that we can address other people in different aspects of their lives and their characters. Often a person's reaction to us depends on our approach and our expectations. This also applies to active imaginings.

In order to use this strategy, we have to know our own fear and apprehensions and know at what point our counterpart might become dangerous to us. Fully conscious of the danger, we then take the risk of addressing this figure in its potentially benign aspect. This isn't a matter of a naïve belief that all interior figures have nothing but good intentions. It is a matter of taking a close look at what threatens us, and then, nevertheless, addressing the potentially good in it.

Resolution by means of confrontation: A good fight requires good preparation. Fairy-tale heroes mostly engage in battles only after a lengthy "quest" or developmental journey, and after passing various tests. Then, mostly at the end of the tale, they find they have to confront a decisive problem—usually the problem that lies at the root of the many problematic situations they have come through—and put up a fight.[80]

Resolution by means of cunning: In order to employ wiles, one has to see through the counterpart's strategies and preempt them. When we're able to use cunning, this always means that we know our own "evil" aspects, hence know how to imagine evil in fellow humans or various figures of the interior image world.

However, we can only use cunning if we don't suffer from excessive fear. An effective ruse is based on a creative idea in the given situation. If we're too paralyzed by fear, our creative imagination is no longer at our disposal.

Flight: If we're unable to mollify figures that appear threatening to us by addressing their benign aspect, and can neither fight nor defend ourselves by means of cunning, we're compelled to flee. In the imaginative context, this very often involves our detaching ourselves from the images, opening our eyes, then mostly talking about what it was that frightened us so much. If necessary, a relaxation image may be employed, and strategies for dealing with the threat may be discussed, before another attempt is made to deal with the situation.

The use of magical objects: In fairy tales, essential transformations—sometimes even expressed as a flight—may be effected by means of magical objects or liquids.

One of the best-known magical objects is the magic wand.[81] It belongs, most often, to a witch, and it may be obtained from the witch's daughter when the latter is running away from her mother: her flight is only made possible by that very same magic wand. The magic wand represents the hope that wishing can effect change, that our wishes change the world, that there always are creative solutions as long as we believe in them and want to bring them about.

In fairy tales, one obtains the magic wand after spending a sufficiently long time in the vicinity of the witch who owns it: we gain the energy to change, the potency to change a situation precisely by subjecting ourselves emotionally to a difficult situation and then, at the appropriate time, deciding to avoid the situation, to no longer remain in a fixed attitude.

Fairy tales also tell us of magic hats that may assist a hero or heroine on their flight, seven-league boots, flying carpets, etc.

It seems to me that these objects can't be employed easily in our active imaginings. They may, of course, be used if the imaginer has been working on a problem for some time and has received these magical objects in the course of his or her imaginative work on that problem. As a therapist, I would not use them in an intervention, since this would strike me as using a trick to overcome a difficulty. If a magical object seems the last resort, I prefer to interrupt imagining, address the problem, discuss strategies, and defuse the fear inherent in the situation by making it clear that we can tackle the threat together. When, however, the imaginer sees and employs these means him or herself, they are entirely acceptable. What we see belongs to us. Some of the magical liquids that recur in fairy tales are closer to our experience than other addressed magical objects are. The healing properties of water play an important part in fairy tales: after blinded heroes or heroines have been roaming through the landscape for a while, someone or some "accident" shows them that the morning dew can restore their eyesight.[82]

In other fairy tales, heroines or heroes find their way to a spring and restore their sight by washing their eyes in its water. The spring water may have other transformative properties: in the fairy tale "Little Brother and Little Sister,"[83] the little brother drinks from a bewitched spring and turns into a fawn. The question is whose domain such a spring may be: is it a good fairy who serves life, or a wicked witch whose master is death?

Tears, too, can restore sight;[84] this experience can be transposed to real life. When we find our way back to our feelings, frequently even feelings of grief, we can see with our hearts again, are no longer blind and hard of heart.

It is a matter of considerable interest that fairy tales stress the transformative power of water. In analytical psychology (which deals with the unconscious) water in general is regarded as a symbol of the unconscious in its various manifestations. Working with the unconscious is seen as opening up possibilities for transformation and hence recovery. We also know that this transformative power of the unconscious may produce undesirable results as well as desirable ones.

We also relate to the healing waters at spas, believing in their curative properties.

Even milk is sometimes found helpful in fairy-tale battles against overwhelming adversaries. In the tale "The King's Son and the Devil's Daughter"[85] the devil's daughter has fallen in love with the king's son who has, in fact, been sold to the devil by his father. The king's son and the devil's daughter decide to flee. After the devil's underlings have lost their quarries twice because they haven't noticed that the devil's daughter had changed her and her lover's shapes, the devil himself sets out as well, but then his daughter changes herself into a pond of milk, and the king's son into a duck swimming in it. She also tells him not to look at the devil, no matter what enticements he may offer. But the duck raises its head a little and causes the milk to ferment—probably because the devil's daughter is turning sour—and the devil, impatient now, starts drinking the milk which goes on fermenting in his stomach and causes him to explode. Devil's daughter and king's son are free at last.

Even in fairy tales, magical objects and liquids don't show up at every turn. Fairy tales don't provide instant wish-fulfillments that would make suffering seem unreal. Until heroes and heroines find the water that heals them, or the water of death and life[86] that joins severed heads and limbs back to their bodies after death and then restores them to life, they have to endure long and arduous quests and odysseys, often despairing but never ready to give up. Only after enduring a difficult situation for a long time can they experience the transformative powers of life.

Opening the circle of fear by intervention: The imaginative technique does not come up with speedy solutions to problems but may provide them, for the first time, with imagery, and thus make it possible to recognize and experience them.

The interior figures we're afraid of are parts of ourselves that make us anxious; often they're images of split-off complexes, aspects of our being that clamor for the co-existence that we are denying them for some reason.

All dealings with interior figures are a matter of integration. In the case of threatening figures, we're dealing with a particularly important integration of parts from which we have become, or have perhaps always been, alienated.

Frequently, they have to be experienced for some time in their fear-inducing aspect. When we consider that they represent parts of ourselves which, becauses they are frightening, we have excluded from our conscious life, we realize it can't be the purpose of the imaginative technique to rashly strip away their frightening quality and turn them into friendly figures all at once. Which is not to say this may not happen, on occasion; but in my experience, they mostly have to be endured and closely observed, exactly because of their oppositional nature toward our consciousness. They must be given space to be imagined, described, expressed. A dialogue has to be created between them and our conscious self, so that we become truly capable of absorbing even these oppositional tendencies, not just in order to rush them into some supposed state of harmony, but with the intention of allowing both sides to unfold in the process—which enables us to know ourselves and our dark sides better.

Once the frightening aspects have been sufficiently accepted for us to allow them to manifest themselves, the tension between our ego-consciousness and those aspects is no longer insufferable but usually already productive.

When, however, fear renders such an interior figure ever more threatening, to the point where it can hardly be approached anymore, an intervention is required. As long as the tension caused by fear is not great enough to trap the imaginer in a circle of fear—mostly represented by a continuous enlargement of the pursuing or threatening figure coupled with decreasing size and increasing helplessness on the part of the imaginer—that tension between the imaginer and the fearsome figure should be maintained. What contradicts and opposes us, in our psyche as well as everywhere else, should not be instantly "co-opted" and stripped of its difference. Oppositional aspects of our being have to begin a dialogue, but they can do this only if they're granted acceptance and respect.

Even in everyday life we tend to make haste to reassure one another that we are really talking about the same thing, sharing the same intention, even though we're using different words. One of our reasons for doing this is that we feel better when we see the world and its problems from identical viewpoints. In many cases it would, however, prove more creative if we let each other know that while we respect and cherish each other, we may not be saying the same thing. After that, each one would be free to expound his or her view, unhampered by the untimely question as to who is "right" in this case. That question has a way of terminating a dialogue,[87] sometimes even before it had a chance to become a creative one. When we deal with each other by means of dialogue, it isn't a question of who is right, but a question of permission to deal with the subject from a variety of angles. To my mind, this is of great importance in imaginative work as well.

Example from Therapeutic Practice

A twenty-four-year-old female student first sought therapeutic help for her process of detachment from her parents. After thirty-six hours of analysis, the problem has receded into the background and mostly resolved itself; now, however, she complains about being afraid of walking in the street. She has a feeling of being pursued by someone, "a kind of tingle down her back," a strange feeling, and she wants to know if she's suffering from a persecution mania.

We agree to work on the problem by imagining. After a period of light relaxation I encourage her to imagine herself, as well as that strange feeling in her back, as vividly as possible. The strange feeling in her back is the symptom she has presented, a symptom she experiences physically, which is why I think it is useful to concentrate on it.

She: "I sense that someone is following me, a very tall young man. I sneak a look over my shoulder. It's a boy from the neighborhood. He is sixteen or thereabouts, much larger than in reality, far more than eight feet tall, and much more muscular—and he has really remarkable teeth, teeth like a vampire. I get frightened, I run, he is much faster, I can hear his breath. . . . "

I intervene by saying: "Turn around, look at him."

She: "I turn around, very abruptly. He is surprised, seems to have lost his bearings somehow. Now I take a closer look at him. I suppose the business with the teeth is a little exaggerated. But he is tall. But not eight feet, maybe seven."

I ask her if she can establish contact with him.

She: "Do you want something from me?"

He: "I'd like to walk with you for a bit of the way."

She considers: What can I do, I really don't want that; but if I don't do what he wants, he'll get huge again. I remember that it is important for me to define my boundaries and to find a place I feel good about. Then I can consider how to deal with relationships.

She: "I was on my way to the . . . café. Would you like to have a Coke with me? I have twenty minutes or so." ("I'm thinking that this is the time of day an older actor frequents this café, I know him well, and I also know that he'll come to my aid if need be.")

He (grins): "Sure, I'd like that, twenty minutes is a big chunk of time. You see, I have a problem: I've just quit school, and my father is incredibly angry with me."

"I get frightened. I don't want to solve other people's problems. Now he looks huge and frightening again. Then I think and say: 'All right, we can talk about that.'"

Then she detaches herself, spontaneously, from these images.

This is an imagining in which it strikes me as sensible to help the analysand by means of interventions to behave in such a way that this interior figure does not become increasingly threatening. She herself already knows a few ways to deal with this fear-inducing interior character.

Typically, we experience what frightens us as "large" and ourselves as tiny in relation to it. This is made figuratively visible in the imagining.

Her imagining clearly shows that the analysand is afraid of this young man who presents his problem to her. It is, most likely, a problem of some significance to the analysand as well.

If we hadn't succeeded in alleviating the threatening quality of the interior figure to some extent, the imagining might have exhausted itself in trying to find some way of dealing with the threat or else fleeing from it; in that case, the problem of which the analysand is afraid would not have come up, and the cause of fear wouldn't have become apparent.

Now we may be able to establish a connection between the imagining and her present life. This young woman is a student both at the local university and at an acting academy. Until now, she has always stated that she's quite capable of reconciling the two different loci of learning; she relaxes from her academic work by acting, and from acting by means of academic work.

I ask her what quitting school means to the boy. The analysand then tells me that he is no longer in school at all, it isn't a question of him, surely more a question of the youthful rebel within herself. For a long time, she has been explaining to me how important she thinks it is to finish one's education; then she has realized that there's a part to her that finds this notion absurd—that must be this sixteen-year-old. She really wants to quit her university classes and just go on with acting, in order to really concentrate all her energy on it. This thought, however, really frightens her, and it, too, is absurd—and when she considers what her father would have to say about it . . .

Her father is of the opinion that she should choose a middle-class profession; later, should she indeed prove sufficiently talented, she could always devote herself to the theater.

The unadmitted interior conflict created fear. As soon as the analysand has spoken about it, she is able to examine it, weigh the pros and cons; she ponders seriously whether this is simply youthful rebelliousness or whether she really could stand by her wish to drop her university studies.

In this situation, it certainly made sense to first of all reduce the fear-inducing factor to normal human dimensions in order to gain access to the problem. It was particularly easy to establish that normal human scale in this case, since the young man was of such superhuman size, and clearly described as such.

It isn't always as easy to decide whether one should, in the case of an imagining with a threatening figure, use interventions to reduce fear, or whether enduring that fear would be more productive.

Often people initially encounter a problem in their imaginings. That problem won't be worked on within the imaginative framework, but—as this example demonstrates—it can be gradually clarified by means of notions that occur in regard to it, connections to everyday life, interpretations, etc.

The Necessity to Endure Fear-Inducing Figures

Example from therapeutic practice: A forty-two-year-old woman (with about thirty hours of analysis), who sought analytical help because she suffers from recurrent depressive upsets, has a dream in which she sees a disheveled, wrapped-up "evil woman." She didn't want to have anything to do with her, but was dreaming about her all night; she kept showing up in the dream.

The dreamer is able to express that the presence of this woman hurts her. She finds it hurtful that such a figure appears in her dreams, that she sees one of her own personality traits in this woman, and it upsets her even more that she keeps thinking about her. None of this fits her self-image: "I don't want to have a disheveled, ragged, evil woman inside of me. And I wanted to get rid of her, all night long—but now, as I'm talking about it here [in the analysis session], she's present again, so I'll probably have to deal with her."

It seems appropriate to use the imagery technique on this dream image that even haunts her by day. It might have been possible to draw a picture of this woman, but that didn't occur to me at the moment. After light relaxation, the analysand imagines the woman. She says: "Surely she's a witch, I'll have to be nice to her, maybe I can give her something to eat"—(with, presumably, the intention of turning the witch into a wise old woman)—"maybe I can take her along and tame her."

The analysand knows many fairy tales, she knows how one is supposed to deal with witches. I ask her to imagine this wild woman.

At first, the analysand finds it very difficult to see an image. That is typical in such a situation: when we're asked to imagine figures we don't like to see, we find it hard to see them clearly in our imagining. This is also true about figures farther removed from ego-consciousness, figures which originate at deeper levels of the unconscious. Thus, it is often difficult to determine whether a poorly perceived image is caused by an entirely legitimate resistance to seeing fear-inducing figures, or whether it is the case that figures existing at a greater distance from our consciousness will appear only gradually. Often we need a period of five to ten minutes of concentration on a poorly defined interior image before the outlines become sharper and the image can really be recognized. Here, representation by means of drawing may be helpful.

The analysand, after about three minutes of concentration on this image which she was at first incapable of defining: "I'm in a region that strikes me as somewhat familiar—indeed, it's the village I come from. I stand by a river, and that's a spot I've always loved and where I still go today when I visit there. The witch is standing closer to the river than I am. I move toward her, she's standing behind a thorn hedge. I say to her: 'You look so pretty there, in the thorn hedge.' (I think, that's *Dornröschen* [Little Thorn-Rose, the German name for Sleeping Beauty] —damn it, I don't want to be Sleeping Beauty.)

"The witch turns away.

"Guess that was too crude, I say to myself. Or is she reacting to my thoughts, and not at all to what I'm saying? So, I try again: 'I like this river. Do you like it too?'

"She turns halfway back to me. She doesn't say anything. Her face is hard, closed, and she looks fierce: cold eyes, compressed lips.

"I look around, see some strawberries. I pick them and think: Well, if she doesn't accept them . . . That's an extremely erotic symbol, she has to take them, I'm sure they taste good too. I offer them to her. She slaps them out of my hand.

"Now I'm very sad, don't know what to do. The woman sits down on a big rock and starts flailing away at the flowers growing around it. Now she's beginning to frighten me. Things aren't going the way I had thought. I feel sorry for the flowers.

"I tell her: 'I feel sorry for the flowers.'

"She: 'I don't. I destroy.'

"I: 'I see that.'

"She: 'I want to destroy.'

"I: 'You want to—you don't have to?'

"She: 'I want to.'

"I: 'I want to destroy.'

"I look at her, at a loss again. She is wearing many layers of clothes, I only just noticed that, she looks quite shapeless. Then I remember hearing it said that clothes are the magic cloaks of concealment for our innermost being. What can she be like, inside? What am I really like, inside, finally? I don't look at her again, stop thinking about her.

"Then she asks me: 'You're leaving?'

"I think, triumphantly: Now I've got her. She is afraid of separation.

"I: 'Yes, I'm leaving.'

"She: 'Then I'll destroy,'

"I: 'I'll come back. I'm interested in you, but I don't understand you.'

"She: 'You torment me.'

"I: '*You* torment me! '

"She: 'You!'

"I: 'No, you!'

"She: 'No, you!'"

I intervene: "Both of you want to destroy."

The analysand starts weeping and detaches herself from the imagining.

In the wake of this first imagining, the analysand conducted a dialogue with this wild woman for several months, a dialogue accompanied by important interior images.

She started the imagining with the intention of dealing with this, to her so unpleasant, woman in an expedient manner. This is also indicated by her decision to declare her a witch, and by her subsequent recollection of what seemed significant to her in dealings with witches. She doesn't succeed in her attempt to reach a quick understanding: this side of her, "muffled up" even in its image, needs time to show itself, to unfold aspects of her being. First of all, it shows itself as a very destructive side. The dialogue soon demonstrates that the analysand also becomes destructive when she has to deal with this destructive side.

In the wild woman, the analysand first of all encounters her own opposite. There is little that's wild about the analysand: she rather gives an impression of excessive domesticity. Cleanliness is one of her highly regarded values, and she finds it hard to deal with the notion that her coiffure might not be impeccable. This is why this figure from her dream is a bit much for her. She is afraid of this aspect but also yearns to be a wilder woman; for the time being, this yearning for wildness is, however, contained.

The wild woman also represents aspects of destructiveness. In terms of the analysand's life history, this wild, destructive woman points to her own mother, whom she experienced as very destructive. Her mother told her that she had made several, unfortunately unsuccessful, attempts to abort her. Thus, the will to destroy has been present in the analysand's life from an early age. Understandably, such an experience, together with the brutal communication of that fact, activates the theme of destructiveness in a person.

I have chosen this example to demonstrate that there are imaginings in which precisely such implacable confrontations have to be endured before the threatening side can show itself—together with the ego and its capabilities of dealing with that side.

On Dealing with Obstacles

Since our active imaginings are often made in situations in which our life appears problematic to us, they frequently depict conflict, and often not yet in the form of real conflict but, initially, just as a blockage of the image flow. Such obstacles very often cause the entire interior image flow to come to a standstill. Hence, strategies of intervention are essential. As it turns out, everybody tends to experience a couple of similar obstacles in their lives.

Mostly the obstacles express themselves spontaneously in images, or we wake up with a dream image that concerns such an obstacle. If we want to know which obstacles are of immediate importance to us, we may choose a particular motif as the starting point for an imagining:

Possible instruction for imagining (after relaxation):
Imagine a brook or a river.
Observe the surroundings through which it flows.
(After a minute or so:) In the bed of this brook or river there are obstacles to the flow of water.
Observe these obstacles closely and see how the water manages to make its way in spite of them.
(After about two minutes:) If you like, try to feel yourself as water, and make your way in spite of the obstacles.

With the motif of flowing water, I have introduced into the imagining the notion that life is a perennial flow, and that there always are obstacles to this flow which may stop it or bring about new ways of flowing. At the same time, I also express the idea that the water, in its motion, ends up being stronger than the obstacles confronting it. The river of life goes on regardless of what the obstacles are.

Here a question arises: What kinds of obstacles are placed in the imagined brook or riverbed? They are related to obstacles one keeps encountering in everyday life, and the way in which the brook or river flows around them lets us draw conclusions about how we habitually deal with obstacles. We may also expect to find, in the course of imagining, a new and creative way of dealing with them.

The feeling the imagined obstacles arouse in us frequently corresponds to our feeling about concrete obstacles in everyday life. It is, however, often easier for us to admit to a particular feeling in the course of an imagining than it is in the course of everyday life.

The feeling experienced in the imagination encourages us to ask ourselves whether we couldn't also have these feelings in corresponding situations in our everyday existence, if only we allowed ourselves to have them.

Example from therapeutic practice: Even without the specific instruction to imagine an obstacle in a brook or river, this image may appear spontaneously as a representation of an obstacle in a real-life situation.

A very depressive male, fifty-eight years old, approaching mandatory retirement, seeks therapy because he has lost interest in life. In cases of depression I favor the river as a motif for imagining, in order to see what may still be flowing in this particular life. Besides, the river motif always has a vivifying effect.

In his spontaneous imagining, the man sees a river high up in the mountains. This river is extremely cold and runs very fast, leaping from one rock to the next.

Suddenly a mountain appears in the river, and the more the imaginer looks at it, the bigger it grows, until it blocks the river's way. The river can't get over or around it; it tries to flow to the right, then to the left, then with all its energy, then more gently, with little pressure—to no avail, it is now jammed into a gorge, it has to start flowing backwards. It doesn't get dammed up, it flows backwards and somehow disperses, trickles away.

The imaginer, surprised and at a loss, falls silent. I ask him: "But where does the water go?"

He thinks for a long while, then says, with a mischievous smile: "The water collects in a subterranean river. The river simply goes on down below."

I: "How do you feel as a river that flows down below?"

He: "Good—I feel good as a river that flows down below—but now it flows very slowly, it can no longer leap about the way it was doing above ground."

This imagining was a spontaneous image sequence on the brook or river motif. I didn't ask the imaginer to construct an obstacle in the river, even this appeared spontaneously: a mountain blocks the flow of the river and forces it to find a new bed. Mountain brooks often have to circumnavigate boulders, but when an entire mountain appears and blocks the way, we think of a major upheaval. We know the expression that there are "mountains to cross."

Asked about the mountain facing him, the analysand starts talking about unfinished tasks that worry him, and about a yearning to pick up many things left aside in the course of his life—those, too, are mountains. He does not volunteer anything about his mandatory retirement, which to an outsider could also be represented by that mountain in the river.

When I ask him about it, he says he thinks that this retirement might improve the quality of his life. He says it is practically normal to be retired early in his profession, one that requires a great deal of responsibility. Then he lists a number of colleagues who have also retired early. He tries to see the situation as a favor from the powers that be. He doesn't mention that he didn't seek retirement but that it was forced upon him from outside.

Hence, he finds his sudden depressive states inexplicable. Only the mountain that appeared in his river so unexpectedly impels him to speak at length about how unjust he feels this early retirement to be, how it has hurt his feelings to be singled out for it. Then he says that life now confronts him like a mountain, and he has to find some way of getting around it.

In his imagining, there is no such way, since the water is flowing in a gorge. Identifying with the water, he must have the impression that his life has been constricted. Considering the gorge, he thinks about his age and about how the paths he has made for himself in this life are "worn smooth" like a gorge. In addition, it occurs to him that he can't see over the sides of the gorge.

In the realm of aging problems, he worries about not having had a real relationship with his wife for a long time, and anticipates great problems in that respect as soon as he will no longer have his job.

His imagining indicates clearly that things can't go on this way. He is—as a river—surprisingly mobile, tries to pass the mountain on the right, on the left, tries to circumvent the obstacle with a lot of energy or gentle persuasion. He has many problem-solving capabilities. The solution, however, is that the river has to flow backwards. He rejects the idea that the water might at some point rise so high that it would flow over the mountain. In his imagining of this process, the mountain would also keep on growing larger.

The imagining shows that it is necessary to turn around, but surprisingly enough the river "trickles away" in its backward flow. The imaginer says that that is how he feels at the moment; he knows the obstacle in his life, he senses that he has to choose a new road, but all his energy trickles away somehow. This is the image of his depression.

Without an intervention, he would have concluded his imagining here, letting the image sequence confirm, as it were, his depression. Initially, my intervention arose out of the image itself: water doesn't just disappear, it is in perennial circulation and has to reappear somewhere. It may change the form it appears in, but it can't really be lost. Thus, energy is not lost in a depressive state—it has to be searched for. Something must be found to stimulate us, however slightly.

The imaginer is obviously inspired by this subterranean river. He uses it to indicate that while his life has gone into hiding, it is still flowing. One might look for this river, but at this point it doesn't strike me as important to do so. What's essential is that he's able to feel the emotion the image of this river managed to release in him—if only for a day, as he tells me later. He had felt himself to be a river, and for the first time had perceived hope that his life could start flowing again. Only after he had sensed this feeling vividly was he able to deal with the mountain ahead of him, the mountain of problems which he has to solve somehow.

He tells me that this image corresponds to his sense of things. On one hand, it seems to him that everything crumbles in his hands, that he has no more strength, energy, impetus—on the other, he also feels that something is alive in him, not so obviously, but nevertheless alive, if only in a far more sluggish fashion than he would like it to be.

Much later in the therapy process, a dream image gave us a reason to return to the subterranean river. At that point it became obvious to him that the subterranean river was, for him, also the river of forgetting, and that this violent confrontation with his age, one he'd been avoiding until then, brought out an image that was meant to tell him the water was now flowing back to its origin, and that he had to deal with the subject of mortality. At the point at which he developed that image sequence, this interpretation was not timely for us. The subject of turning back, in general, was central, and, above all, his experience of still being part of the flow of life, even though the current had been reversed.

Imaginings depicting obstacles, as they often do, are particularly vulnerable to stoppages unless one succeeds in intervening in a way that makes it possible to deal with the images.

Imagining as Depiction of a Crisis

Interventions can also raise obstacles represented in imaginings closer to consciousness, making it easier for the imaginer to deal with them and to establish their connection to everyday life.

A twenty-two-year-old male, with no previous history of psychological problems, sought help at a time when he was required to take an intermediate examination, saying he felt confused and unable to deal with the exam. This was a matter of crisis intervention.[88] In a crisis intervention, the task is to find out which realm of life really is experiencing a crisis and what changes are necessary. Only rarely is the situation that triggers the crisis really the reason for the crisis in a person's life.

I ask the student to imagine a river or a brook in which there is an obstacle. (For directions, see p. 134.)

"I see a river, thirty to forty feet wide, green meadows. The current is swift, the course of the river is nice and straight, no bends in it at all. Now, suddenly, everything freezes. All the water freezes."

As he says this, his body becomes very tense, and his voice expresses horror.

"That's impossible, in a river. Very deep down it is still flowing a little."

I ask him to examine the image calmly and in detail.

"No, it's frozen—congealed by the cold."

The student sighs, opens his eyes, appears quite helpless.

This is an image of his situation, and it can be worked on. Quite often the difficulty will be represented by one image, one obstacle, before any sequence of images can arise.

In a therapy situation I try to see the imaginer's images as vividly as possible. I let the imaginer describe them to me. I, too, am bound to react to the situation with my own notions of these interior images as soon as I can't really perceive them, i. e., don't have the necessary information. In order to empathize, I have to submit to this image world as far as possible, but at the same time, and over and over again, I have to distance myself from the emotions triggered by that world, if I want to know when to intervene.

I have mixed feelings about this particular imagining. At first, I am impressed by the relatively wide stream and see it flowing along in my imagination, rather slowly; then I am shocked by the sudden, very dramatic freeze.

I ask the imaginer what has caused it/him to congeal.

"Fear of the exam."

My own association was rather a disappointment in a relationship.

He responds that he did have a girlfriend but things hadn't worked out, she always found fault with him, it was all over as far as he was concerned—and no big deal. He isn't going to see her much anymore. He has to prepare for his exams.

When I ask him how the situation appears to the woman, he says everything seems to be all right with her.

I ask him to re-imagine the congealed river and ask him whether there is any hope for it or whether it will have to remain frozen forever.

He is able to re-imagine the river, senses the cold, and says that he himself is feeling like the river—motionless, cold, and empty.

Any hope for it?

"Well, a whole lot of people could show up and start chopping up the ice."

I ask him if he can see these people showing up and chopping up his ice.

No, he can't see that, that had just been an idea. But he could of course wait until it got warmer, wait until spring.

I don't find either one of these possibilities appealing. In the first one, the imaginer simply wants to remain passive and have others do the work for him; in the second, he has to wait, and that is impossible in his present situation.

I ask myself if this young man perhaps isn't rather indolent, with a tendency to lapse into the role of a child asking others for help when confronted with a circumstance in which success does not seem unquestionably assured. I also consider the extent to which he concentrates only on himself in the context of his problem. I'm a little surprised by his statement that the whole situation won't cause any further problems for his girlfriend. Or is he really so frozen that he really can't come up with any ideas of his own, or any energy to work on his situation in order to change it?

To gain clarity about these hypotheses, I ask him to describe the surroundings of the river. The image should make it clear to what extent this young man's present life has come to a halt.

He describes the surroundings of the river as lush and green. This lush green meadow suits him—he gives the impression of a young man in whom the sap is still rising.

Once again, I give him my interpretation of the ice, saying it may have to do with an emotional trauma, and tell him I think he's now telling himself: "Let others try to get me going again."

He receives this interpretation with a smile.

I ask him whom he is punishing with this seemingly insurmountable exam.

"My girlfriend, of course."

And as he says that, he says to himself: "Oh, I just hate it when I play the victim."

When I ask him what kind of a river he would find totally satisfying, he says:

"Livelier than the one I saw at first, wilder, maybe even wider—with a really fast current."

Then he tells me, spontaneously, that he hates bends in the river because these impede the flow of the water. It also seems to him that such a bend might slow one down when kayaking on a river. His fears connected with river-bends are significant. Although he has only told me about these, not seen them, I have the impression that he perceives himself in a kayak at the bend of a river, incapable of taking that turn, adjusting course, and that this is the reason why he feels so upset about the bend.

He is unable to share this view. He insists that when he sees images, he always sees that frozen river again. It's possible that he avoids seeing himself in a kayak at the riverbend because that image would turn the problem into his problem and affect his self-image to a much higher degree than the image of the frozen river.

It is also possible, however, that it was I who transformed his story into an image, the image that seemed to express his situation to me—the rejection of which caused him to freeze. One may also assume that he was transferring the fear of a frozen river onto a possible bend in it.

Since this interpretation, which I didn't tell him about, struck me as plausible, I decided to introduce an imagining centered on a relaxation image, in order to give him some relief. He had already told me that he had a lot of trouble sleeping. When people are able to concentrate well on a relaxation image they find significant, this may have a positive effect on their quality of sleep. Hence it seemed important to me to find a relaxation image for him, and to practice it with him, so that he would be able to use it as an imaginative exercise at home.

After a relaxation period, I gave him the following directions:

Imagine a body of water in which you would like to take a dip.
How warm should it be?
How large would you like it to be?
In a building or outdoors?
If outdoors, select the degree of cleanliness of the water, and the weather that seems right for a swim.
Then just lie down in this water, enjoy it.
You don't have to do anything, just enjoy.
You can't sink, either.

After waiting a minute, I asked him to get out of the water, take a refreshing shower, then open his eyes and detach himself from the images.

The imaginer sees a warm, steaming hot spring in Iceland, about two meters across. He enters it and says: "I can really relax here, I stretch, dream myself into the sky. . . ."

Suddenly he interjects: "But what do I do with my head, I have to hold it up, otherwise it'll sink under the water. But if I have to hold it up, I can't relax completely."

I suggest he place a swimming belt, one like children use, around his neck. He likes the solution. He becomes more relaxed again, doesn't say much for a while, then:

"I'm dreaming myself into the sky, it's nice and warm, I feel secure."

I tell him to imagine this image in the evening, before going to sleep, as vividly as possible for half an hour or so.

It is, of course, more to the point to let imaginers develop their own relaxation images, but since this young man was in a crisis, I gave him motifs from relaxation images that occur very frequently. His reaction showed that the image "fit" and that he was able to see images that relax him.

Three days later, at our next appointment, we returned to the river motif. When a single image depicting the problematic situation occurs, it makes sense to look at that image again in order to establish what changes may be reflected in it.

This time he sees a river that is about fifteen feet wide, still flowing through a very green landscape, the grass even seems a little taller. The water surface is still frozen, but he thinks he can hear a glugging water sound.

It seems to me that he is asking me, in the language of images: "Will you be able to make this ice melt today?" I ask him: "Is the ice breaking up?"—indicating that I don't intend to start chopping the ice.

He doesn't say anything for a while. Then: "Now I have two feelings that are quite different from one another."

I ask him to visualize these two discrete and different feelings in two images.

"I see myself double."

"How?"

"I see an iced-over man, and a man in a tennis outfit."

"How would you describe the iced-over man?"

"He is burdened, pressured, constricted."

"And the one in the tennis outfit?"

"He is light, strong, seductive. He makes an impression on women."

The conflict expressed in his contradictory feelings, and initially seen in the image of the river that flows at first and then freezes, has now been brought to a level closer to him. He sees himself double, in contradiction, but he is able to look at himself.

I suggest he let both these men address a sentence to his girlfriend. I base this on the assumption that his disappointing relationship to her might be his main problem, and that the two types of men perhaps represent different attitudes toward the girlfriend. It would, of course, also be possible to see the types as images of transference, in which case his relationship to me may have brought out the two men in him and made it possible for him to experience them.

The iced-over man tells the girlfriend: "I am so burdened, I feel quite alone, I can never love again. I'm not loved, and therefore I want to be a living reproach to you."

He finds it harder to identify with the young man in the tennis outfit and speaks of him from an observer's point of view: "He talks to her, acts charming, now he turns and says, There are other women, you know."

I ask him whether these two types could start a conversation between them. He says that's not possible.

Then I ask him to have them call each other names. It is my intention to get the two self-images into a dialogue, since they seem to represent widely divergent possibilities of behavior, each one of which, by itself, may be too lopsided.

The iced-over man says to the man in the tennis outfit: "You show-off, you Don Juan, you miserable phony—you really aren't, you'd just like to be that way." And the tennis guy to the iced-over one: "You little martyr, you guilt-monger, you blackmailer, you howling misery."

It becomes evident that the student can identify much more intensely with the iced-over man. He regards the man in the tennis outfit as a wishful image, as a possibility of compensation for the present difficult situation. The relationship of the two sides is a hostile one.

I go on to ask whether both of these figures really are so thoroughly unsympathetic—whether they don't have any positive possibilities for their lives.

"Well, the tennis guy has a good sense of his body, and good self-esteem. He believes in the future. But he's also really dishonest, a phony."

At first, he can't see anything acceptable in the iced-over man. "He's just really stupid, the way I am when I feel insulted, I just withdraw, just like my father used to do, and my grandfather. One just becomes non-aggressively aggressive, no one says a word, but the atmosphere gets really heavy and ice-cold. I don't like that reaction, but I do react the same way."

He can't see anything acceptable in this figure. I point out that there has to be a human being under the coat of ice, which surely is just a kind of protective armor. He says it could be a sensitive, impressionable man with feelings he can not stand by, and this makes him become ice-cold.

I ask him to put his disappointment with his girlfriend, and his anger towards her, into words. He has clearly said that the iced-over man is unable to express anger and disappointment, being passively aggressive.

Quite surprised, he says to me he doesn't know what anger I'm talking about, and that I have totally confused him now.

I decide to let him return to the relaxation image we practiced in our previous session.

In a subsequent session we continue work on this problem. His confusion has to do with my translation of the problem clearly addressed by the image to everyday life; this triggers more fear, and he has to protect himself against that fear.

In the next session, after another four days, he tells me he is sleeping better thanks to the relaxation images. His work is also proceeding a little better, but he has to do something about his girlfriend. He says he went to see her and acted like a sulky clod. At school he has tried to make her jealous by flirting with a couple of other girls. She has told him he was acting like a stubborn child, and now he feels very hurt again.

I ask him to concentrate on the river image again.

"Now the river is about twenty feet wide. The surface is

still frozen, but it is flowing underneath."

Then he sees nothing more, and I get the impression that we're still stuck.

Then I get the idea of a journey in time.

The Journey in Time

At times when we feel the pressure of a great workload we console ourselves by thinking that the task will be done in three or four weeks. Then, more or less consciously, we imagine what life will be like after that. We also console one another by pointing out that "things" will get easier after a while.

In childhood, we often engage in imaginings that have to do with time: "When we are grown-ups at last." We imagine what it might be like when we've transformed the weakness that makes us yearn to grow up soon, into a strength.

We know from experience that deeply depressing experiences are no longer so depressing once a sufficient length of time has passed.

Certain experiences, very embarrassing and painful at the time, may provide amusing anecdotal material a few weeks later. It's one thing to be caught in a difficult situation that makes us feel helpless, another to have overcome that difficulty and to be able to judge the situation from another point of view which allows us to see its amusing aspects, the comedy of it, with our regained sense of humor.

These are the insights we use when going on a journey in time. In an extremely oppressive situation, we try to gain the point of view we'll probably have in a couple of weeks, or months, or years, when we think back. But even when we are not in a difficult situation, such a journey in time may show us new perspectives. We can, for instance, imagine how we'll be living ten years from now, how we will look, how our bodies will have changed, where we'll be, what work we'll be engaged in, what interests we will have then. A journey in time demonstrates the imagination's ability to project the future, and sometimes it shows us aspects of our being we haven't been thinking about. We allow the journey to reflect ludicrous forms of our existence, exactly because it is a game.

The technique of time travel can also present the consequences of various possible decisions. If one receives two offers and can't decide which one would suit one better, one may imagine how one will be living in three years' time if one accepts one or the other. The very fantasies one may have about various decisions and their consequences show us which hopes and fears we associate with the various offers, and the offer that makes our fantasies livelier is probably the one that attracts us more deeply.

Our sense of reality may create difficulties on this journey in time. We really have to allow ourselves to proceed freely into the future. We may argue that many things we can't yet know might affect all the projections. That is undoubtedly true—but the purpose of a journey in time is not to represent the future as it will be but as I imagine it now. We use such counterarguments only when we find ourselves unable to play the game of travel to the future. A childlike lightness of heart is what we need for such journeys.

If, on the other hand, we find ourselves besieged by nothing but misgivings on such a journey, we have to stop those images, proscribe them, perhaps refrain from ever using the time travel technique again.

Possible direction for imagining: First I point out, once more, that if negative images occur, they have to be stopped. Then, after a brief period of relaxation:

Concentrate on something that feels like a burden, that both-

ers you, that you find difficult to deal with.

It doesn't have to be the greatest problem in your life. Try to perceive the feelings connected to this problem.

Also be aware of your body.

And now you realize that you can manipulate time. . . .

Imagine time.

Try to see what all that now is burdensome, bothersome, or difficult to deal with looks like three weeks from now.

Try to see how you can deal with it.

Put aside negative thoughts. You may get used to the problem, but no more than that.

Now it is six months later.

How does the problem look now?

How does it look in a year's time?

How does it look in five years?

Then detach yourself from the images but don't abandon your immersion yet; perceive your feelings one more time, exactly.

Now I want to introduce you to another form of journey in time.

Remember once again the river or the brook with its obstacles.

If you haven't seen one yet, imagine one now.

Now observe the flow of the river much, much farther down, far below the obstacles.

Perceive your feelings again.

Then, slowly, detach yourself from the images.

The second kind of journey in time is made in more symbolic form. The advantage of such a more symbolic journey is that we find it easier to admit the images, and that they won't be allowed to trickle away immediately but will have to be interpreted.

There are, of course, problems that won't have undergone any essential change in five years' time, and toward which our attitude won't have changed to any essential degree. There also are problems that will become more acute in a few years' time. When someone has just been confronted with the diagnosis of a possibly life-threatening illness, the future may still bring a full life despite that illness, but it may also bring death.

The method of time travel is less suited for deeply significant existential problems than for problems of the moment which depress us and which we tend to overestimate, out of a certain sense of panic.

Back to the example: The problem that doesn't want to change and that I want to address with the journey in time, is the problem of the "lump of ice" that stubbornly refuses to melt because the analysand can't admit to himself how hurt he is inside of his armor, how much he suffers from having been abandoned.

I ask the analysand: "How will the lump of ice look in three weeks' time?"

"It'll have to work hard not to thaw."

"Is it working hard?"

"No, it's too much trouble."

"If the lump of ice thaws, what does that mean?"

On this occasion I keep my questions on the symbolic level. I have found out that the young man is capable of describing his problems very precisely on this level, but as soon as we leave it and ask ourselves what these images might mean in actual life—thus, also inquire about possible consequences—he reacts defensively.

He then explains to me the thaw would mean that he would have to admit his positive feelings towards his girlfriend, and also this feeling of fear of abandonment. It has already frightened him to realize how dependent he is on her, how miserable he would feel if she left him. And she is such an independent sort, he might not be able to survive that.

The particular hurt to his feelings, he now finds out, was caused by her telling him that he acted either like a jovial phony or like a stubborn infant. This occurs to him when we ask ourselves what has happened to the man in the tennis outfit.

In subsequent imaginings he practices, over and over again, a clarifying conversation with his girlfriend, in which he tells her how much this remark has hurt him because he feels that it wasn't unjustified.

This, too, is a way in which we can use imaginings—but relationships can also be represented and experienced on a more symbolic level, where closeness and distance as well as the nature of the relationship may become apparent.[89]

Essential for the student in this imagined conversation was that it became clear to him how poorly he'd been able to empathize with his girlfriend until then. He found it hard to imagine what she would tell him in reality.

The imagery technique may be used to practice empathy with another person—but it is, once again, important to allow this other person to truly speak her or his own language. We must not simply put our own words in his or her mouth.

Imagining as Dialogue with the Body

CHAPTER TWELVE

JUNG POINTS OUT that the formation of symbols is often associated with psychogenic physical disorders. He bases this well-known observation—which can be extended to mean that we may not see a symbol in the figurative sense but merely a physical symptom—on the hypothesis that "the unconscious is the psyche of all the body's autonomous functional complexes."[90]

The phenomenon can also be understood in terms of a complex, as defined by Jung. The essential thing about a complex is the emotion associated with it, which in turn creates the conditions for certain behavior patterns that remain the same. Emotions always have a physiological correlative. Very early on, Jung contributed to the holistic psychosomatic view of the human being which has been envisioned by a number of other authors and has become common property in the consideration, experience, and evaluation of health and illness.[91] This view doesn't apply only to psychosomatic illnesses in the strict sense but also to the fact that the human being, understood as a whole, can always be seen as a system in which psychic, somatic, and social factors interact, so that problems on one level may also express themselves on another level.[92]

Hence, we may regard physical as well as social symptoms as symbols. We can let physical symptoms depict themselves and then work on these images, as we work on those dream images that remain in our consciousness.

The flow of interior images may start out from physical perceptions. The body in general may represent the motif around which we create our imaginings.

One way of establishing imaginative contact with the body consists in making a journey through it, visiting our organs, trying to perceive what they look like, finding out if they need help, etc.

This kind of imagining may stay close to the reality of the body's anatomy, but it can also be made fantastic by means of imaginative visions of the various organs. The more fantastical these imaginings become, the more they reveal about our organs and our relation to them.

Instead of making a journey through the entire body it is also possible to establish contact with a particular part of the body. We are most likely to do that when something is hurting and we wish to find out what the body has to tell us.

Possible direction for imagining:
After light relaxation, I ask a person who can feel a symptom to concentrate on it, to observe the tension and the feelings associated with it, and to wait for an image to arise out of this tension. Often there is an image in place as soon as I ask the person to concentrate on the symptom.

Example from Therapeutic Practice

A forty-three-year-old man suffers from stiffness of the neck. It feels just like a pinched nerve but has persisted for six months. This very active man practices a responsibility-laden profession, is successful in it, has a family, and everything is going quite well—except for this neck pain.

We decide to work on the symptom by imagery. We go through a few relaxation exercises, concentrating, as always, on the body part to be imagined later.

I urge him to feel his way into his stiff neck. He says:

"I get two images. One is an ox yoke, and in the other I see myself as a circus acrobat: on my shoulders and neck I carry a chair balanced on a pole. Another person jumps onto that chair."

Thus, he is the one to carry the chair. I ask him how he feels. He says:

"It is a cramp, and I am terribly tense."

I ask him if there is anything he can change, and he says:

"Not really, or at best I could change places."

But before he changes places in his imagination, he says: "No, I have another solution. I can lie down."

He lies down and says: "Well, right behind my head there's a hole in the arena, and I can just stick the pole into it. I don't have to carry that stuff anymore."

Lying down, he feels completely relaxed.

There we have an example of how a symptom can be expressed in images. These speak for themselves: being yoked, and what's more, like an ox. On the subject of the ox he says that oxen are the world's greatest working beasts. That's one of the possibilities, and the other is that of the circus acrobat. He has never had anything to do with the circus although he loves it—but he also has the feeling that it is a place where people show off, so that, somewhere, he must also feel like someone in the arena where everybody is watching and waiting for peak performances. He has the following notions about the life of acrobats:

"Acrobat . . .That's inherited, from one generation to the next; that's one of those lives one is simply born into, and in which one simply has to achieve peak performance."

Then he relates this to his own life by saying: "That was certainly the case in my family, peak performance was expected, from my father before me, and if I don't watch out, my sons will probably feel the same pressure."

I ask him what comes to mind considering the carrier figures in the circus.

"They're mostly the fathers [he himself is a father of four children]; big strong guys, although they're always trembling with the effort. The one at the bottom really bears the brunt of it, but no one gives him any applause."

Again, he establishes the connection to his life: "I put a lot of effort into my work, and get a lot of applause for it in my profession, but at home no one pays any attention, they see it all as a matter of course. It's a matter of course that I 'huff and puff,' and only when I say I want to pack it in the whole family starts yelling and wants to know if that means the ski vacation has to be called off."

Thus, the neck tells us quite a few things. The man whose neck it is feels harnessed, perhaps even subjugated. On his neck sits a family that doesn't applaud him for working so hard but is also unwilling to accept it if he works less. Here, "family" may refer to his actual family, but it may also be the family inside him that can't accept a slackening of his pace.

In his imagining he has found a possibility for relief: he has discovered that it is possible to simply plant that pole in the ground.

I want to know who it is he has to keep up there in the chair and ask him to try to imagine that person.

He says, very quickly: "That's me again sitting there, in my best position, as it were."

He has to support himself in his best position. He is forty-three years old and knows that he is in his "best years"—this means, of course, that there won't be any better ones.

Now that he has imaginatively succeeded in ridding

himself of pressure while maintaining himself in his special position, to what extent has the tension in his body been relieved? When working on images emanating from physical tensions, the question of transferability can be studied better than in images with other motifs.

After this man had completed this imagining—which lasted twenty-five minutes—he sat up and found it considerably easier to turn his head, with more freedom of motion to the right than to the left.

Even a relatively brief imaginative engagement with a symptom may provide relief. Therapists who use body-work or breath therapy may object that imagining is superfluous: relief is achieved by having the person concentrate on a part of the body, which causes the circulation to improve in it and thus makes it more mobile again.

Even if it were only the concentration on the afflicted organs that brings about an improvement, I would never want to miss the information inherent in an image that stimulates one to further engagement with the situation. The image is a basis for insight.

For these symptoms to appear as images, the ego's control function has to be abandoned to a great degree. It is either handed over to a therapist, as is often the case in these imaginings, or else one's confidence in the ego's control function is so great that it can be relinquished for the time being.

In the first case, the imaginer surrenders to the interior images and trusts the therapist to intervene when necessary, whenever the imaginer can't find his or her way out of an impasse. The more practice people have with the imaginative technique, the more they've experienced what kinds of intervention are possible, the more likely they are to trust themselves to have ideas which will help them manage even difficult situations, in other words, to trust the ego's control function.

Who uses the imagining method without the help of a therapist will either succeed in having the stress depicted in an image or sequence of images, or the pain will remain dominant as pain, i.e., no images will be perceived. It goes without saying that it is possible, even on one's own, to relinquish control to the extent that images begin to appear.

Imagining in Functional Illnesses

Many different theories attempt to explain why there are people who react to conflicts primarily with physical ailments, others mainly with psychic disturbances, and still others who become embroiled in social difficulties.[93]

There is a relative consensus that people who suffer from frequent functional ailments have problems perceiving and expressing their feelings, both their own and others', in a differentiated way. Psychosomatics do not have fewer feelings than other people, but they do have trouble admitting and expressing them.

Since psychotherapy works with emotions, the obvious question arises whether the difficulty psychosomatics have in expressing their emotional state verbally also manifests itself on the image level—whether, as has been claimed, psychosomatics really are "unimaginative," think only in concrete terms, and are limited in their ability to experience things.[94]

Wilke presents a study in which his work with guided imagery on patients with colitis ulcerosa and Crohn's disease—classic psychosomatic illnesses—is described and investigated.[95] He maintains that the patients treated and examined by him are not limited in their expressive capabilities on the image level. He does, however, point out that psychosomatics find it difficult to delegate the controlling ego to the therapist, and that they tend to prefer concrete imaginings for a longer time than other patients.

Hence, it is particularly useful to employ relaxation images and to work with various strategies of intervention with such clients.

Wilke also states that with psychosomatics suffering from ulcerative colitis and Crohn's disease the creation of images of symbiosis and nourishment (relaxation images), which he himself calls images of regression, is extremely important and effective. He finds a more rapid recovery in patients who are able to imagine such regressive images. These are images of the positive/nourishing mother arche-type, and they point to the fact that we have to look for the genesis of psychosomatic afflictions in a very early stage of human development, at the point where this archetype is first constellated in a child's evolution.

Behavioral therapists also investigate which basic need has not been satisfied in the development of a person suffering from a particular psychosomatic ailment, and encourage the person to keep imagining an image that is congruent with this basic need. Thus, Lazarus[96] cites one of Ahsen's cases, a twenty-eight-year-old woman who was hospitalized for acute ulcertive colitis, had to defecate fifteen to twenty times a day, the stools consisting of blood, slime, and water, and whose organic processes were unstable. He asked her to imagine seeing herself as an infant, hugged and cuddled by her mother. Apparently, this imaginative exercise stabilized the vital signs of this woman within twenty-four hours.

This report, bordering on the sensational as it seems, may indicate that nourishing relaxation images are of great importance in the treatment of psychosomatics. It does, however, seem more sensible to me to let them find their own images, the ones they need and find helpful.

In my work with psychosomatics I try to lead them from the image they have of their symptom into contact with the symptom and the body in general. I consider the development of relaxation images and their use of great importance.

Example from therapeutic practice: A thirty-seven-year-old man has already consulted several physicians. He has had a heart attack and now panics at the possibility of another one.

In functional cardiac problems, an important part is played by the memory of the singular experience coupled with the fear that the experience might repeat itself. Hence, we speak of cardiac phobia. There is great fear of and anxiety about another attack.

This man describes his heart attack: "I felt extremely restive, then my heart was racing, then my pulse rate felt like after an eight hundred meter race—I've always been an athlete and am therefore very sensitive to such physical changes, especially in the heart—then I broke out in a sweat, flushed, and had great difficulty breathing. But that wasn't the worst of it: the worst was this absolute fear of death, the feeling, the idea that my heart was going to stop any minute now, and it would all be over. And I thought, dear God, all the things I missed out on in life, and so much still left undone."

These thoughts must have intensified his fear. It is typical of the emotion of fear that once one is gripped by it, one has further thoughts and notions which intensify it, and the result is a circle of fear. The man now suffered from tremendous fear of another attack and had himself examined several times in order to find out what might be wrong with his body. He tried all kinds of things, various diets, exercise plans, etc., but was unable to shed the fear, and started taking things easier and easier.

At the beginning of therapy, in which he invested little hope—he just didn't want to leave anything untried—I asked him to create an image of his heart. He said:

"I see an alarm clock. It's ticking regularly, and suddenly it starts going wild and then stops."

And: "I'm sure you've seen that happen with those old alarm clocks—all of a sudden, their hands start whipping around the dial, and then they stop."

That was how he saw the situation. He couldn't come up with another image but went on talking about his fear. He told me his life story and described his present life. I tried to empathize with his fear as far as I was able. Slowly he developed a degree of trust in me.

After about six months of analysis he told me that he had once again, in the evening preceding our session, tried to create an image of his heart, the way we had tried to do at the very beginning. This time, he had seen the heart as a small heartperson: a tiny figure shaped just like a normal human being but only about two inches tall, dressed in a red sweat suit.

Then he said: "And this little heartperson controls my heart. I can't do anything about it."

This was the therapeutic moment to generate a dialogue with the symptom: when the symptom appears in human shape, this is indeed an invitation to engage it in human discussion—provided, of course, that the analysand no longer simply delegates the problem to the body.

Here is an excerpt from this analysand's dialogue:

He: "I'm so afraid of you, heartperson."

Heartperson: "I know."

He: "I'd like you to tell me what you have in mind."

Heartperson: "I never have anything particular in mind. So I can't tell you. You have to find out for yourself."

He: "But that's what I've been doing all this time. All I do is fantasize about my death."

Heartperson: "But that isn't what interests me."

He: "What interests you?"

Heartperson: "Life interests me, effort interests me,

being moved interests me, an involvement with life interests me."

He: "But it's you who prevents me from that."

Heartperson: "You think so?"

This exchange repeats itself.

Among its other functions, fear serves to show the
affected person that something that wants to share his or
her life is not permitted to do so. Precisely by manifesting
itself, however, fear—from a certain point onward—prevents anything new from being created. This pernicious
chain is reflected in this dialogue.

In this situation, it is advisable to concentrate on a relaxation image and then to undertake an exchange of roles
with the symptom. I ask him to imagine a situation in
which he might feel particularly good.

His image: "I see myself windsurfing, it is warm, the
lake not very big, two to three points on the wind scale,
nothing to worry about, but a steady wind. I flit effortlessly across the water and experience once again how
great it is, the water spraying onto me, the wind. My wife
is watching me from one shore, waiting for me, and my
kids are swimming by the other one, they keep looking to
see where I am. Everybody is having a good time."

The analysand visibly relaxes while watching these images. His idea surprises him, he hasn't been windsurfing
for several years, afraid it might prove too much of an
exertion.

This image sequence shows clearly that it would be
important for him to develop a greater degree of autonomy, albeit in a very protected atmosphere: members of
his family are waiting for him on both shores, but he is
able to separate himself from them a little without feeling
separated. He points out that this arrangement pleases
the entire family, that it does not give rise to any aggressions. The relaxation image addresses the need to work on

the problem of separation[97]—which often occurs in cardiac phobias—and resolves it for him.

After this relaxation image has calmed him down, I ask him, without discussing the image with him, to change roles with the symptom. I ask him to enter into the skin of the heartperson.

He: "I feel great as the heartperson. I wield uncanny power over this Hugo [his imaginary first name]. It's a joy to feel his fear and trembling. All I have to do is go a little faster, and he's afraid. Then he tyrannizes everybody, starts writhing about, it gives me great satisfaction. That Hugo doesn't understand anything about me. It's true that I want peace and quiet, but I want excitement, too. I want to be excited in a nice way. I want him to live with me, with his heart, not just his head. But I've resigned myself, there's nothing you can do with him."

In the role of the heartperson, this otherwise extraordinarily courteous, endearing, friendly man reveals himself as a sadist.

I ask him whether he could speak to himself, Hugo, in the role of the heartperson.

The heartperson tells Hugo: "Now listen, let's just put an end to all this fuss. You coddle yourself the wrong way, you don't have to take it easy, taking it easy is going to kill you. Just gather up your courage at last and launch yourself into life."

Hugo: "That's all very well and good, but, heartperson, it's you who keeps me from doing that"—(his tone is obsequious)—"I'm simply at your mercy. Whenever I do something daring, you start beating faster."

The heartperson growls and says: "I'm not satisfied with you at all. You could suggest a compromise—you could suggest doing something, and I agree not to beat too hard."

Hugo: "No, no, I'm afraid to suggest that to you."

The heartperson, the personified symptom, behaves sadistically, and Hugo plays the masochist's part, lets the symptom subjugate him completely. Even when the symptom lets him know that it is willing to make a compromise, relinquishing the sadistic role with that suggestion—an indication that such a degree of masochistic submission isn't necessary—he doesn't dare.

This also points out how hard it is for this man to gain confidence, which was made manifest by the considerable time our joint efforts took before he even dared to give in to his images.

The symptom and its surroundings: A symptom has a function within the relationships in our lives. Hence my question: To whom is the symptom addressing itself? I leave open the question which member of the family it is that the symptom wants to speak with. If I get the impression that people are passed by in silence with whom the relationship is problematic, I give more definite instructions, such as, "Let the symptom talk to your wife."

Hugo sees the heartperson in his family: "Now I see the heartperson walking around our apartment, invisible, influencing everybody even when they aren't saying anything and even when he isn't saying anything. Everybody pays attention to the heartperson as if he were the most important head of the household.

"My wife says, 'I can't discuss problems with you, they might be the death of you.'

"Suddenly, the heartperson plants himself in front of her and tells her: 'You must never leave him alone, else he'll die. You have to protect him always.'

"My wife says, 'I'm tired of that. I don't want to do it anymore! Who is protecting me?'

"And the heartperson suddenly starts dancing all over her, and my heart beats much faster.

"She says, 'I won't be blackmailed.'

"Now my heart beats even faster.

"She starts fixing my [i.e., Hugo's] pillows, she gives me

the necessary protection again, and the heartperson calms down."

The action of this imagining is probably similar to what happens in real life. After thinking it over for a while, Hugo says: "That's really nasty. With this symptom, I exercise total control over my wife." Then he leans back a little and says: "It's not just nasty, it's also very practical."

To the children the heartperson says: "When you broach a subject that doesn't suit me I'll stamp my foot a little, and you'll feel guilty right away. I can make you feel guilty anytime, but I won't make you feel too guilty, because then you might leave."

The subject of separation occurs over and over again in these imaginings: the heartperson wants to produce just enough of the symptom to keep everyone there, but no more, because if he were left alone, what then . . . ?

Then the heartperson speaks to Hugo's father and mother, a conversation we can skip here. Finally, he speaks to the boss: "You, sir, you thought that this good-natured person would take care of all the work you don't want to deal with, you wanted to make him your deputy. Now he has to be handled with care. He's no longer any good for a managerial position, and that isn't his fault at all, it's fate. Don't burden him with anything. You can't fire him, either. Who could fire a sick man who still contributes good ideas?"

The heartperson has many functions: he has made Hugo's wife comply with his wishes, he attaches the children to him, saves him from the excessive ambition which might have led him to a position he might no longer be able to handle. In addition, the heartperson makes him feel good about it; he can't help it that he can no longer advance, he is a victim now, a victim of illness. In its own way, the symptom really behaves like a sadist, like an attacker, and Hugo is the victim, but that isn't all there is to it—he gains something as well, and the persons he relates to become victims.

When one identifies with the symptom, one expresses the fact that this attacker is part of one's own psyche. One is both victim and attacker. Then problems have to be dealt with on a much broader basis, problems of aggression and separation have to be perceived and worked on.

In dealing with symptoms it becomes apparent, time and again, that the symptom, and illness in general, is seen as an "attacker" and the person as a victim of this attacker. This shows that we tend to operate on the premise that we'll always be healthy. We experience illness and, in that connection, death, as a disturbance against which we are helpless.

This attitude makes our initial dealings with the symptom take on the character of a power struggle: either the symptom or the bearer of the symptom has to win or lose. These dealings become productive only after the symptom is no longer fended off, when it can be seen as something belonging to life, the way even death is ultimately part of our lives.

Active Imagination

CHAPTER THIRTEEN

IN JUNG, the concept "Active Imagination" covers every rendition of a symbol, be it a visual continuation of a symbol in the imagination or, more descriptively, a painted picture or sculpted representation. Initially, even rendition by means of dance was termed Active Imagination.

It seems important to me to remember this comprehensiveness of Jung's sense of the Active Imagination, even though, with the passing of time, only the development of an imaginative picture in a waking state, and an active examination of this image, has been termed Active Imagination.

Jung mentions Active Imagination for the first time in 1916 in the essay "The Transcendent Function" [98] in which he describes the theory of symbol formation. In this essay, Jung does not explicitly discuss Active Imagination but concerns himself with the question of how people concentrate on their fantasies and how they are able to shape them. In that context it strikes him as particularly important to eliminate critical awareness. Here, Jung mainly stresses the importance of waiting for, perceiving, and recording these images or interior words,[99] expressing and describing them with one's hands or the whole body.[100]

Jung writes about the Active Imagination a little more extensively in his essay "Anima and Animus." [101] He also talks about it in his introduction to Richard Wilhelm's *The Secret of the Golden Flower*.[102] Here he still stresses that the art of letting things happen in the psyche is a prerequisite for Active Imagination (which is still not designated by those words). This letting things happen in the psyche is identical with "letting flow" the interior images. It isn't all that easy to let it happen—fear inhibits the flow of images. Jung says repeatedly that we have to disengage our critical faculties during imagining. In my opinion, however, we can also let the critical aspect, the critical voice be rendered and take its place in the imagining.

Even in the already cited description of 1941 (see p. 18), in which Jung uses the term "Active Imagination" and gives the specific instruction to concentrate on an interior image and then wait for the flow of images, he is basically still speaking of the perception of fantasies. But here, in contrast to, say, his descriptions in "Anima and Animus," where he is concerned with hearing what these figures have to say, the emphasis is more on the image.

Then, in a letter written in 1947, Jung describes succinctly what he understands as Active Imagination:

> The point is that you start with any image . . . contemplate it and carefully observe how the picture begins to unfold or to change. Don't try to make it into something, just do nothing but observe what its spontaneous changes are. Any mental picture you contemplate in this way will sooner or later change through a spontaneous association that causes a slight alteration of the picture. You must carefully avoid impatient jumping from one subject to another. Hold fast to the one image you have chosen and wait until it changes by itself. Note all these changes and eventually step into the picture yourself, and if it is a speaking figure at all then say what you have to say to that figure and listen to what he or she has to say. Thus you can not only analyse your unconscious but you also give your unconscious a chance to analyse yourself,

and therewith you gradually create the unity of conscious and unconscious without which there is no individuation at all.[103]

In this description of Active Imagination it becomes apparent that it involves perception of the interior image as well as verbal dealings with interior figures. It can also be seen that the model of symbol formation, as described by Jung,[104] can be moved into the realm of experience by Active Imagination: the unconscious shows itself, has to be perceived and accepted, and in the dialogue with consciousness, the waking ego, both consciousness and the unconscious are transformed and may be experienced in changing symbols or new symbol formations. These symbols are milestones of the individuation process, which involves becoming, by means of the dialogue between consciousness and the unconscious, the person one really is, always on the way, and more and more oneself.[105]

This is expressed vividly in a letter from 1950:

You must step into the fantasy yourself and compel the figures to give you an answer. Only in this way is the unconscious integrated with consciousness by means of a dialectical procedure, a dialogue between yourself and the unconscious figures. Whatever happens in the fantasy must happen to *you*. You should not let yourself be represented by a fantasy figure. You must safeguard the ego and only let it be modified by the unconscious, just as the latter must be acknowledged with full justification and only prevented from suppressing and assimilating the ego.[106]

Jung admits, however, that even just the free flow of fantasies may have a liberating effect on the patient.

Ability to control, on one hand, and the ability to let the images flow, on the other, are the prerequisites for Active Imagination. The difficulty of the process consists in the necessity of having the ego give in, time and again, to the flow of images, so that the ego relinquishes a great deal of control and thus allows these interior figures as much autonomy as possible; but thereafter, in an entirely changed, wakefully conscious attitude, the ego has to deal with these figures and thereby shapes and formulates what it has seen and surmised, before it once again abandons itself to the flow of images.

The "active" in Active Imagination involves the ego's active entry into imagining, its "controlling" and transforming/metamorphosing role in the imaginative event. This connects the unconscious to our consciousness.

Passive fantasies are fantasies, image sequences which are basically always with us, the ceaseless river of the imagination of which we are (or are not, occasionally) aware. Passive fantasies may also be fantasies that attack us and against which we can't defend ourselves. We are then determined by an affect, a complex with its specific emotion and attendant behavior patterns, and we're not able to deal with it, but are at the mercy of our emotions and images. The complex may show itself more in terms of emotion or more in terms of a sequence of images. In this situation, we feel bereft of our freedom, determined by outside forces.

Passive and Active Imagination

An example to make the distinction: Shortly before she was due to take her school-leaving exam and university entrance qualification, a young woman got married and then never took this important final exam. She became a mother and hausfrau. Now, at the age of forty-six, she seeks therapy because she is asking herself what is to become of the rest of her life. She tells me repeatedly:

"Something inside me tells me, over and over, that I've done everything wrong in my life: married the wrong man, at the wrong time, chosen the wrong life-style, etc." I ask her to give this "something inside me" a shape. Her imagining: "I see a judge in a black robe, bald like my grandfather, wearing glasses like an uncle of mine, with a face with those sharp features typical of sadistic people.

He is taller than I, stands on some kind of elevation. I am totally at his mercy, and he tells me these familiar sentences. I'm ashamed, I squirm with shame. I should have noticed all those things myself. I apologize and vow to improve myself immediately."

I stop her with the remark: "This won't succeed." I ask her to immerse herself into one of her relaxation images. She does so and feels a little better again. Then we discuss her imagining.

This is an instance of a passive imagining: the analysand is completely at the mercy of the interior judge. The interior figure, a composite of many traits of authority figures she has known in her life, gives her a piece of his mind, the analysand squirms with shame and wants to improve herself immediately. She has, however, vowed to do so for many years, without success; hence, my intervention is designed to indicate that I regard this intended "improvement" as an illusion. She really had no idea in what ways and in which concrete situations she wanted to improve, she only had a generalized will to great improvement, which couldn't be dealt with in this degree of abstraction but would have to be approached by small, concrete steps.

In a conversation subsequent to this passive imagining we deal with the question whether the words of the judge make any sense at all. We note that he uses words like "always" and "everything wrong": this makes us feel rather skeptical, since always is never, and since it is very hard to do everything wrong.

We also discuss the question what empowers this interior judge to make such findings about her life, and what her arguments in favor of her own life are. Without such arguments, she surely would have changed her life a long time ago. We clarify why it is that she assigns such great importance to the judge, even places him in an elevated spot and sees herself as insignificant next to him.

Then I suggest another imagining, but one in which she takes an active part with her ego. I suggest dealing with the dissatisfaction of the judge.

He is so reproachful he has to be dissatisfied. In a case like this it may be far more productive to address the dissatisfaction than to feel shame as a victim of that dissatisfaction.

The analysand (A.) to the judge (J.):

"You're very dissatisfied with me."

J.: "You do everything wrong. From the very beginning—wrong decisions, wrong choices. You just don't have your head on straight."

A.: "Why are you using the familiar form of address (*du*)?"

J.: "I've always done that. Go ahead, you can call me *du* as well."

A.: "No, I don't want to do that. Let's use the formal (*Sie*)."

J.: "As you wish. It doesn't change the fact that you are a failure."

A.: "Does that bother you so much?"

J.: "It bothers me a great deal. I had such great hopes for you. True, you're just a woman, but you could have made something of yourself with your intelligence. But you were so lazy."

A.: "That wasn't laziness, it was passion."

J.: "It was laziness, fear, and maybe even passion. But one might live passionately and still pass exams."

A.: "I can see that, today."

J.: "And what is your excuse now?"

A.: "Always fear, not so much laziness. I'll never be good enough for you."

J.: "You'll learn to endure that."

The analysand and the judge have resumed the informal address. The dialogue continues in this manner and goes on for weeks. The interior judge becomes more precise, thus more tangible. He addresses individual aspects she would be able to change if she so desired. However, it becomes obvious to her that there are certain respects in which she does not want to live according to the demands of this interior judge, and that she is capable of justifying this. He also demonstrates that she regards women, even herself, as inferior. She finds this appalling. Gradually she detaches herself from a very destructive authority complex. By dealing actively with this complex, she gains—although she still feels helpless in many ways—a feeling of not being at its mercy, and soon the complex becomes less destructive. This diminishes her own destructiveness towards herself.

On this level, one relatively close to consciousness, an Active Imagination is being created that changes the analysand's consciousness. It also changes the unconscious: with time, the judge acquires friendlier traits. His face becomes a little more rounded, and in his verbal manifestation he even admits to not having an opinion on a certain situation.

The wrangling about the form of address ceases in the first imagining in which the analysand speaks about experiences that have existential significance for her. It may be that she gains some initial distance from the judge by refusing the *du* and consciously defying him.

Active Imagination—as is apparent here—brings us into a dialogue with our unconscious, a dialogue that can be used to change both conscious and unconscious aspects. It replaces a sado-masochistic relationship, expressed in this instance by the fact that the interior judge has jurisdiction over the woman's ego. Only when the ego has no means of resisting the unconscious—or has so little structure, is so weak, it can't be active—can the unconscious have such an overpowering effect.

This also shows the limits of this method which follows the principle of the creative process: the method requires a well-structured ego that can stand up to the uncon-scious. One cannot expect such a well-structured ego in every imaginer, which is one reason why I have indicated a way in which the image flow can be practiced by means of training the imaginative faculty in general.

Furthermore, I have tried to demonstrate how, in the therapeutic process, the therapist may assume the ego function of the analysand. A learning process then enables the analysand to deal with these interior figures, and the ego's ability to control is strengthened. This, in turn, makes it possible to detach the ego complex from the parental complexes, to distinguish between I and not I, to facilitate an examination of these aspects. As paradoxical as it may seem, it is precisely by means of this examina-tion, made possible when the analyst puts his or her ego functions at the analysand's disposal, that the analysand's ego structure can be improved and strengthened; this results from its experiencing the ego complex, detached from the parental complexes as befits the person's age, as increasingly more coherent. A good sense of identity arises out of this: the ego is no longer restricted in its func-tions, and defense mechanisms can be employed in a modulated fashion appropriate to the situation.

Example from Therapeutic Practice

Generally speaking, active imaginings will be made with images arising from dreams or emerging by concentrat-ing on one's mood, on an affect that disturbs one, with which one would like to be able to deal or at least discover what problems are hidden within it. There also are direc-tions that can lead us to an active imagining.

Possible instruction for imagining:
Choose a landscape with a body of water.
Someone or something is approaching you. Perceive this

figure, observe it closely.

Establish contact with it:

What does this figure have to say to you, by its manners, its behavior, its appearance or its words to you?

React to these things the way you would otherwise react in an encounter.

A thirty-five-year-old woman who has been in analysis for about a year because she always feels so anxious and listless, works frequently with imaginings. She feels very restless within herself, although initially no reason for this can be found. I give her the above instruction but also ask her to concentrate on her restlessness. Her imagining:

In front of me I see a spring, I'm in a hilly landscape, in the Piedmont, there are trees. It is just a regular spring, and next to it, on a rock, sits an old man, a very old man with a long white beard. His face bears a very serious expression. He looks at me seriously and searchingly.

I approach him and notice that I'm feeling ashamed. I try to find out why I feel ashamed.

I don't know, I come up with nothing but nonsense. The old man looks at me searchingly, and whenever anyone does that, I feel ashamed. I approach him slowly and sit down on the other side of the spring. He goes on looking at me searchingly.

I say: "When you look at me so searchingly I feel guilty, I think I've done something wrong."

The old man nods. He says, murmuring: "That's right, there's always something one does wrong. One has to be like the water from the spring, always flowing, always flowing."

I strain to think what I have done wrong.

The old man says: "Always flow, always flow."

I stop trying to find out what I've done wrong, I relax, feel the spring, the peaceful atmosphere. I look at the old man. He is obviously concentrating on the flow.

Suddenly I discover that there is another man by the spring, a much younger one, an arrogant type in a dark three-piece suit.

He looks at me with an ironic expression.

The guy infuriates me.

He says: "Yes, yes, let it flow, let it all flow, that's right, let life flow by, sit by the spring, sit there until Judgment Day—let it flow, don't take responsibility for anything." He says this with an incredibly disdainful expression.

"How do you dare drag my experience of this spring through the dirt?"

"I haven't thrown any dirt in the spring."

"But you mocked me."

"It's your business if you feel mocked."

He is right, but I have to shut him up. I'm incredibly angry. I have no idea how to stop him. I want to shake him but he is much bigger and stronger than I am. When I get furious I can only think of violence, but he is stronger, I can't silence him that way. Nor do I have a rock I could throw at him.

Now he's looking at me again with that sarcastic expression.

Looking for help, I look over at the old man, he should help me. But he is gazing at the water with great concentration, at the spot where the water leaves the ground.

I do the same. I can feel my rage subsiding, I force myself not to look at the sarcastic guy again. I concentrate on the flow.

After a long while, I look up. I look into the face of the old man, it is quite calm and collected—and the spiteful arrogant one is gone.

I walk away, knowing that the old man will guard the spring, I can return here whenever I want.

I feel pleased and hurry into town.

During and after the imagining the analysand is very impressed by this old man, his concentration, his presence. But she is also happy because she succeeds in concentrating on the flow of the water, and thus on what is essential.

The image became a determinant even in her everyday life. Whenever she felt ashamed again because she had done something wrong, she was able to call up this image.

In her imagining, however, she isn't affected only by this one strong, peaceful image, she is also disturbed by a man whom she perceives as arrogant. He embodies an aspect of her that wants to take a more active part, to take on more responsibility. In the imagining, he does not appear merely critical; his arguments could be quite important, she hasn't yet reached an age in which one may withdraw from the world. But he belittles experiences that are important to her, and thus becomes an aspect of her that turns arrogantly against herself. She wants to deal with him, but brute force doesn't seem to be the way to do it: what works is her concentration on the image of the water as it emerges from the earth, this symbol of energy flowing from the dark interior of the earth up to the light. It makes her experience a feeling of self-being, and out of this secure feeling of being alive she can and will sort out things with her active, energetic side, in an imagining she creates two months later.

At the moment, this concentration on the motion of the water appears essential, and the spring also awakens in her the feeling of being alive, of beginning, origin, and the idea that the water is inexhaustible—confidence in the flow of life.

Concluding Remarks

Time and again, Jung cites Active Imagination as the method that enables one to deal with confusing affects. It also has great importance in the imaginative processing of dream images. In that processing, particular emphasis is put on the final aspect of the symbols, the aspect of expectant hope, of new ideas.

Even "trial actions" can well be performed within the framework of Active Imagination.

This does not exhaust the significance of Active Imagination. When it is employed repeatedly—and imaginings can continue over a long time—we give our psyche an increasing number of possibilities to unfold. Abysses open up in us, we recognize where our life or our ego is endangered, but we also recognize which interior figures are helpful and even fascinating. Furthermore, Active Imagination always gives us the impression that this interior world can be, and even has to be, shaped by us.

In this context, I have to admit that I don't like the word "compel" that Jung uses when he says one has to compel these interior figures to give an account of themselves. The expression may be helpful in clarifying the method of Active Imagination, but what is most essential in the concept of Active Imagination is its dialogical nature—the notion that the unconscious is able to change consciousness and vice versa. If, however, the ego wants to compel those figures from the unconscious to do something, it may easily happen that our consciousness once again violates the unconscious. Active Imagination is not a matter of violation but of transformation by means of dialogue.

Jung has recommended work with Active Imagination particularly for the final phase of an analysis, as providing a chance for the analysand to gain independence from the analyst, to deal with the unconscious more independently.[107] Instead of the analyst who analyzes the unconscious, the analysand's ego now analyzes the unconscious.

That this method was considered so connected to the conclusion of an analysis may be another reason why it is regarded as so difficult.

Jung also used the method by letting analysands engage in Active Imagination at home, record it, then bring their notes to the analytical session.

At an advanced stage, this procedure is quite possible, and is customarily employed in that manner by analysands. However, I consider it sensible and helpful to first employ Active Imagination in an analytical session, to allow the analyst to assume the ego's role whenever this appears necessary.

Besides, once active imaginings have been described in writing, they often lose much of their emotional vividness.

Preliminary stages of Active Imagination within the therapeutic relationship may also be experienced as an impressive creative process that takes place between analyst and analysand: it provides the analytical relationship with a very particular depth, since the joint processing of images within both participants also brings to life deep images in their own psyches.

I believe, nevertheless, that even this stage is temporary and has to be abandoned when it's time to do so. The objective is to enable the analysand to assume the controlling part in Active Imagination him- or herself, to conduct this interior dialogue without external assistance. But it seems very useful to me to ensure that the two essential techniques of which Active Imagination consists, the letting-the-images-flow and the ability to control these images and to enter into a dialogue with them, are initially practiced by two persons.

When employed this way, Active Imagination doesn't lose any of its aspect of freedom and autonomy—on the contrary: only when we've learned to imagine these images by all senses possible, only when we've learned to practice strategies for dealing with tricky situations, will we be able to allow the interior images to unfold in peace without a need for hasty intervention or correction. We are then able to trust that the images won't simply carry us off but that we can work on and with them.

The various techniques I have presented, which may give the impression that an intrinsically extremely free-form method has been put in a straitjacket, serve only the cause of freedom—and may and should be forgotten again as soon as our imagination and our ability to process it has come alive.

Even the numinous character that such active imaginings may have is not diminished by this gradual approach to Active Imagination. Time and again, we encounter contents in our imagination that connect us to the depth of our psyche, that may have a religious quality. On the other hand, we'll always also deal with imaginings close to our concrete everyday world. We have to accept whatever impulses present themselves to us in any given process.

Even when it has become clear that the Active Imagination in its holistic sense—also expressed in the connectedness of right- and left-hemisphere thinking that inheres in it[108]—of letting-flow, of figures, of dialogue that changes its participants, may become a goal of imagining, it still seems important to me to point out, here at the end, that all preliminary stages to this kind of imagining are essential. Even here it's a matter of choosing the form of imagining that seems to us the most appropriate for our particular psychic situation.

The longer I've been working with imaginings, the more convinced I've become that it is, first and foremost, the concentration on these interior images, this collected presence that we experience when we concentrate entirely on our images, that changes the images, and changes us as well.

NOTES

1. Cf. G. K. Mainberger, "Imagination." In *Die Psychologie des 20. Jahrhunderts*, vol. XIV, edited by G. Condrau.

2. M. Frisch, *Andorra*.

3. D. Katz, *Gestalt Psychology*, pp. 21 ff.

4. Cf. J. Singer, *Imagery and Daydream*, pp. 175 ff.

5. J. Segal, quoted ibid., p. 176.

6. "Psychologists have hitherto failed to realize that imagination is a necessary ingredient of perception itself. This is due partly to the fact that that faculty has been limited to reproduction, partly to the belief that the senses not only supply impressions but also combine them so as to generate images of objects. For that purpose something more than the mere receptivity of impressions is undoubtedly required, namely, a function for the synthesis of them."
   From I. Kant, *Critique of Pure Reason*, p. 144.

7. J. C. Eccles in K. R. Popper and J. C. Eccles, *The Self and Its Brain*.

8. Cf. V. Kast, *Das Assoziationsexperiment in der therapeutischen Praxis*, pp. 16 ff.

9. J. Eccles, "Imagination and Art." In *Internationale Gesellschaft für Kunst, Gestaltung und Therapie*, Mitteilungsblatt 4, May 1987.

10. G. Bachelard, *The Poetics of Reverie*.

11. H. Corbin, *Creative Imagination in the Sufism of Ibn Arabi*.

12. C. G. Jung, *Letters 1*, p. 460.

13. See also J. L. Singer and K. S. Pope, eds., *The Power of Human Imagination*.

14. R. Desoille, *Le Rêve éveillé en psychothérapie*.
    H. Leuner, *Lehrbuch des Katathymen Bilderlebens*.

15. V. Kast, *Sisyphos*.

16. C. G. Jung, "The Psychological Aspect of the Kore" (1941). In *The Archetypes and the Collective Unconscious, CW 9/1*, p. 190, paras. 319 f.

17. Cf. L. F. Van Egeren, B. W. Feather, and P. L. Hein, *Desensitization of Phobias: Some Psycho-Physiology Propositions*. In *Psychophysiology*, 1971, vol. 8, pp. 213–28.

18. Cf. H. Leuner, ed., *Katathymes Bilderleben*.

19. "Most imagery procedures are more effective if one first achieves a state of general muscle relaxation. Two different relaxation procedures are outlined: (a) alternate tension-relaxation exercises, and (b) sensory relaxation training. Try both types and see which one you prefer. You might ask someone with a pleasant voice to read these instructions into a casssette recorder, or make your own recording. Perhaps you and a good friend can take turns in reading these relaxation exercises to one another. Once you get the hang of it, just do the exercises from memory. You do not have to adhere to an exact sequence.

ALTERNATE TENSION-RELAXATION

Sit down or lie down in a comfortable position. Take in a few deep breaths, in and out, and let your body become loose and pleasantly heavy. Now try to tense every muscle in your body. Tense up every muscle. . . . Now let go of the tension. Let go and switch off all the tension. Notice the feeling of relief. . . . Let's do that again. Tense up every muscle . . . hold the tension . . . relax, let go, ease up, and enjoy the relief. . . . Take in a deep breath now and hold it . . . right in, breathe deeply in . . . and exhale, breathe it all out, and feel the tension going out of the body. . . . Just continue breathing normally, in and out. Each time you exhale, every time you breathe out, feel the tension going out of your body. . . . Now relax the rest of your body, but clench your jaws and close your eyes very tightly. Jaws are tense. Eyes are tight. . . . Keep the rest of the body relaxed, but study the tense feelings in the jaws and in the eyes and face. . . . Relax the jaws and stop tightening up your eyes. Let the jaws and the eyes and the face relax with the rest of your body . . . enjoy the contrast. . . . Now push your head back until you feel tension in your neck. . . . Shrug your shoulders, lift them up. Your neck and shoulders and your upper back should feel tense. Keep the rest of your body relaxed. Study the difference between the tension in your neck and back and the relaxation elsewhere. . . . All right, relax your shoulders, drop them gently down, and let your head return to a comfortable position. Enjoy the sensations and let yourself relax even deeper. . . . As you relax the rest of your body, tighten your fists and also tighten your stomach . . . try to get tension in your hands, your arms, and your stomach. . . . Study that tension. . . . Let go of it. Ease up and allow the tension to disappear. . . . Finally flex your buttocks and thighs, and point your toes downward so that your calves tense up. Feel the tension in your hips, buttocks, thighs, and calf muscles. . . . Keep the rest of the body relaxed. . . . Every part above the hips is relaxed; feel the tension only in and below the hips. . . . And now stop tensing, relax, ease up, and allow the calm sensations to develop and spread. Relax your entire body. As you inhale think the word 'in' silently to your self, and as you exhale think the word 'out' to yourself. Carry on relaxing like this for as long

as you like, gently and easily breathing in and out.
(Sensory relaxation training adapted from the work of Drs. Bernard Weitzman, Marvin Goldfried and Gerald Davison.)"
The quote is from A. Lazarus, *In the Mind's Eye*, pp. 193–95.

20. J. R. Cautela and L. McCullough, "Covert Conditioning: A Learning-Theory Perspective on Imagery." In J. L. Singer and K. S. Pope, eds., *The Power of Human Imagination*, pp. 227–54.

21. H. Leuner, ed., *Katathymes Bilderleben*, p. 75.

22.

Right Hemispheric Thought	*Left Hemispheric Thought*
Subdominant hemisphere	Dominant hemisphere
Control over left side of body	Control over right side of body
Almost no connection to consciousness (link via the corpus callosum to the left hemisphere)	Connection to consciousness
Almost nonverbal	Verbal
Musical	Linguistic description
Responsive to image and pattern	Ideas
Combining according to visual similarities	Combining according to concepts
Temporal synthesis (concurrent)	Temporal analysis (sequential)
Holistic, imagistic thought	Analysis of detail
Geometric-spacial	Arithmetic and computer-like

From V. Kast, *The Nature of Loving*, p. 97.

23. Cf. V. Kast, *Märchen als Therapie*.

24. H. Leuner, ed., *Katathymes Bilderleben*, pp. 50 f.

25. K. D. Schultz, "Imagery and the Control of Depression." In

J. L. Singer and K. S. Pope, eds., *The Power of Human Imagination*, pp. 281–307.

26. Cf. also A. Sellberg, "Persönliche Erfahrungen mit dem Katathymen Bilderleben in Schweden." In H. Leuner, ed., *Katathymes Bilderleben*, p. 251.

27. J. C. Eccles in D. R. Popper and J. C. Eccles, eds., *The Self and Its Brain*.

28. A. T. Beck, "Role of Fantasies in Psychotherapy and Psychopathology." In *Journal of Nervous and Mental Disease*, 1970, vol. 150, no. 1, pp. 3–17.

29. Cf. R. Ammann, *Traumbild Haus*.

30. H. Leuner, ed., *Katathymes Bilderleben* and R. Desoille, *Le Rêve éveillé en psychothérapie*.

31. H. Phillipson, *A Short Introduction to the Object Relations Technique*.
    W. J. Revers, *Der thematische Apperzeptionstest (TAT)*.

32. On the entire subject, see H. Hark, *Traumbild Baum*.

33. Cf. K. D. Schultz, "Imagery and the Control of Depression," loc. cit., p. 289.

34. Cf. V. Kast, *The Creative Leap*.

35. C. G. Jung, "The Psychological Aspect of the Kore," loc. cit., p. 190, para. 319. Quote rearranged by the author.

36. J. R. Cautela and L. McCullough, "Covert Conditioning," loc. cit., p. 236.

37. On the entire subject, see K. Anderten, *Traumbild Wasser*.

38. G. Riess, *Traumbild Feuer*.

39. E.g., G. G. Márquez, *Love in the Time of Cholera*.

40. Regarding the selection of fairy tales as well as different methodologies, cf. V. Kast, *Märchen als Therapie*.

41. In *Russische Volksmärchen*, selec. and tr. by Xaver Schaffgotsch.

42. This is a fairy tale of the animal groom type. Cf. "Das singende springende Löweneckerchen" ("The Lilting, Leaping Lark" in *Grimms' Tales for Young and Old*) in V. Kast, *Mann und Frau im Märchen*.

43. J. Sandler, "Gegenübertragung und Rollenübernahme." In *Psyche 4*, 1976, pp. 297–305.

44. M. Ermann, *Die Gegenübertragung und die Widerstände des Psychoanalytikers*. Forum Psychoanal. Heft 2, 1987. C. G. Jung, "The Psychology of Transference." In *CW 16*. M. Jacoby, *Psychotherapeuten sind auch Menschen*. V. Kast, *The Creative Leap*. J. Sandler, "Gegenübertragung und Rollenübernahme."

45. See "Allerleirauh" ("Thousandfurs" in *Grimms' Tales for Young and Old*) in V. Kast, *Familienkonflikte im Märchen*.

46. Cf. A. Lazarus, *In the Mind's Eye*, pp. 150 ff.

47. S. Freud, *Introductory Lectures on Psycho-Analysis*, p. 372.

48. S. Freud, "Creative Writers and Daydreaming," p. 146.

49. Cf. E. Bloch, *The Principle of Hope*.

50. Cf. J. Singer, *Imagery and Daydream*; and J. Singer and K. Pope, eds., *The Power of Human Imagination*.

51. C. G. Jung, "Problems of Modern Psychotherapy" (1929). In *CW 16*, p. 56, para. 125.

52. C. G. Jung, "The Feeling-Toned Complex and Its General Effects on the Psyche," in *The Psychogenesis of Mental Disease*, *CW 3*, pp. 38–51.

53. C. G. Jung, *The Structure and Dynamics of the Psyche*, *CW 8*, pp. 34 f., para. 63.

54. See direction for imagining.

55. Cf. V. Kast, *Traumbild Wüste*.

56. J. R. Cautela and L. McCullough, "Covert Conditioning," loc. cit., p. 242.

57. Ibid., p. 243.

58. In this context, Leuner speaks of principles of direction. The principle of reconciliation, the principle of nurture and enrichment, exhaustion, and diminution, the principle of the magical liquid. In *Katathymes Bilderleben*, pp. 41 ff.

59. On this, cf. H. Maass, *Der Seelenwolf*.

60. "Der Kamerad." In *Norwegische Volksmärchen*, ed. by K. Strebe and T. Christianse.

61. "Rothaarig - Grünäugig." In *Kurdische Märchen*.
    Cf. V. Kast, *Wege aus Angst und Symbiose*.

62. Cf. "The Longing for Love without Words" in V. Kast, *The Nature of Loving*, pp. 18 f.

63. See "The Water of Life" in *Grimms' Tales for Young and Old*.

64. See "The Golden Bird," ibid.

65. E.g., "Der Soldat und die schwarze Prinzessin" in *Deutsche Märchen seit Grimm*, ed. by P. Zaunert.

66. E.g. in "The Golden Bird," op. cit.

67. See "The Water of Life," op. cit.

68. Cf. M. Pouplier, *Traumbild Fisch*.

69. Cf. V. Kast, *The Nature of Loving*.

70. In *Grimms' Tales for Young and Old*.

71. Cf. also "Marja Morevna" in A. N. Afanasev, *Russian Fairy Tales*.

72. See, e.g., "Die Blume des Glücks." In *Zigeunermärchen*.

73. Cf., e.g., "The Lilting, Leaping Lark" and "The Fisherman and His Wife" in *Grimms' Tales for Young and Old*. They are discussed in V. Kast, *Mann und Frau im Märchen*.

74. "The Frog King or Iron Heinrich," ibid.

75. "The Water of Life," ibid.

76. C. G. Jung, *The Practice of Psychotherapy*, CW 16, p. 46, para. 99.

77. E. Neumann, *The Great Mother*.

78. Cf. "The Devil with the Three Golden Hairs" in *Grimms' Tales for Young and Old,* and its discussion in V. Kast, *Der Teufel mit den drei goldenen Haaren.*

79. Cf. V. Kast, "How Fairy Tales Deal with Evil." In M. Jacoby, V. Kast, and I. Riedel, *Witches, Ogres, and the Devil's Daughter.*

80. Cf. "The Two Brothers," op. cit.

81. Cf. "Darling Roland" in *Grimms' Tales for Young and Old,* and V. Kast, *Märchen als Therapie.*

82. Cf. "Das weiße Hemd, das schwarze Schwert und der goldene Ring." In V. Kast, *Märchen als Therapie.*

83. "Little Brother and Little Sister," in *Grimms' Tales for Young and Old.*

84. Cf. "Rapunzel," ibid.

85. "Der Königssohn und die Teufelstochter." In *Deutsche Märchen seit Grimm,* op. cit.

86. Cf. the Russian fairy tale "Marja Marevna," op. cit.

87. H. L. Goldschmidt, *Freiheit für den Widerspruch.*

88. On general problems and possibilities of crisis intervention, cf. V. Kast, *The Creative Leap.*

89. Cf. "Making a Commitment to Life While Living with Leave-Taking" in V. Kast, *A Time to Mourn,* pp. 123 ff.

90. C. G. Jung, "The Psychology of the Child Archetype" (1940). In *CW* 9/1, p. 172, para. 190.

91. T. Uexküll and W. Wesiak, "Wissenschaftstheorie und psychosomatische Medizin." In R. Adler, ed., *Psychosomatische Medizin*.

92. Cf. hereto also: "The ego-complex in a normal person is the highest psychic authority. By this we mean the whole mass of ideas pertaining to the ego, which we think of as being accompanied by the powerful and ever-present feeling-tone of our own body. The feeling-tone is an affective state accompanied by somatic innervations. The ego is the psychological expression of the firmly associated combination of all body sensations." From C. G. Jung, "On the Problem of Psychogenesis in Mental Disease." In *CW 3*, p. 40, paras. 82 f. Thus, when body movements, such as the jiggling of a foot, are restrained, the emergence of very important fantasies may be observed, given that one concentrates on oneself in this situation.

Cf. hereto also: J. L. Singer and K. S. Pope, *The Power of Human Imagination*.

93. See T. Uexküll and W. Wesiak, "Wissenschaftstheorie und psychosomatische Medizin," op. cit.
E. Overbeck, *Krankheit als Anpassung*.
H. H. Studt, ed., *Psychosomatik in Forschung und Praxis*.
W. Bräutigam and P. Christian, *Psychosomatische Medizin*.
E. Petzold and A. Reindell, *Klinische Psychosomatik*.

94. H. H. Studt, R. Frank and D. Vaitl, "Alexithymie." In H. H. Studt, ed., *Psychosomatik in Forschung und Praxis*.

95. E. Wilke, "Diagnostische und theoretische Aspekte der Arbeit mit dem Katathymen Bilderleben bei Patienten mit Colitis Ulcerosa und Morbus Crohn." In H. H. Studt, ed., *Psychosomatik in Forschung und Praxis*.

96. A. Lazarus, *In the Mind's Eye*, pp. 153 ff.

97. See T. Uexküll and W. Wesiak, "Wissenschaftstheorie und psychosomatische Medizin," op. cit., pp. 503 ff.

98. C. G. Jung, "The Transcendent Function" (1916/1957). In *CW 8*, pp. 67–91.

99. Ibid., p. 83, para. 170.

100. Ibid., p. 83 f., para. 171.

101. C. G. Jung, "The Relations between the Ego and the Unconscious" (1928). In *CW 7*, pp. 121–241.

102. R. Wilhelm and C. G. Jung, *The Secret of the Golden Flower*.

103. C. G. Jung, *Letters 1*, p. 460.

104. Cf. "The Transcendent Function," op. cit.

105. Cf. M. L. von Franz, "The Individuation Process." In C. G. Jung, *Man and His Symbols*.

106. C. G. Jung, *Letters 1*, p. 561.

107. Cf. M. L. von Franz, "Aktive Imagination in der Psychologie C. G. Jungs." In Bitter, *Meditation in Religion und Psychotherapie*.
M. L. von Franz, "Die aktive Imagination bei C. G. Jung." In Bitter, *Praxis dynamischer Gruppenarbeit*.
M. L. von Franz, *C. G. Jung*.

108. See V. Kast, *The Nature of Loving*, p. 97.

Bibliography

(English originals and translations of works are cited whenever they could be obtained.)

Afanasev, Aleksandr N. *Russian Fairy Tales*. New York: Pantheon, 1976.

Ammann, A. N. *Aktive Imagination: Darstellung einer Methode*. Olten: Walter, 1978.

Ammann, Ruth. *Traumbild Haus*. Olten (Switzerland): Walter, 1987.

Anderten, Karin. *Traumbild Wasser: Von der Dynamik unserer Psyche*. Olten: Walter, 1986.

Bachelard, Gaston. *Poetics of Reverie: Childhood, Language and the Cosmos*. Boston: Beacon Press, 1971.

Beck, A. T. "Role of Fantasy in Psychotherapy and Psychopathology." *Journal of Nervous and Mental Disease*, 1970, vol. 150, no. 1.

Bloch, Ernst. *The Principle of Hope*. 3 vols. Cambridge: MIT Press, 1986.

Bräutigam, Walter and Paul Christian. *Psychosomatische Medizin*. Stuttgart: Thieme, 1981.

Cautela, Joseph R. and Leigh McCullough. "Covert Conditioning: A Learning-Theory Perspective on Imagery." In Jerome L.

Singer and Kenneth S. Pope, eds. *The Power of Human Imagination*. New York and London: Plenum, 1978.

Corbin, Henry. *Creative Imagination in the Sufism of Ibn Arabi*. Bollingen Series 91. Princeton: Princeton University Press, 1969.

Davidson, D. "Transference as a Form of Active Imagination." In *Technique in Jungian Analysis*. The Library of Analytical Psychology, vol. 2. London: William Heinemann Medical Books.

Desoille, R. *Le Rêve éveillé en psychothérapie. (Essai sur la fonction de régulation de l'inconscient collectif.)* Paris: P.O.F., 1945.

Deutsche Märchen seit Grimm. Ed. Paul Zaunert. Düsseldorf and Cologne: Diederichs, 1963.

Eccles, John. "Imagination and Art." In *Internationale Gesellschaft für Kunst, Gestaltung und Therapie*, Mitteilungsblatt 4, May 1987.

Eccles, John and Karl Popper. *The Self and Its Brain: An Argument for Interactionism*. New York: Routledge, 1984.

Ermann, Michael. *Die Gegenübertragung und die Widerstände des Psychoanalytikers*. Forum Psychoanal. Heft 2, 1987.

Freud, Sigmund. "Creative Writers and Daydreaming." In *The Standard Edition of the Complete Psychological Works of Sigmund Freud (CPW)*, vol. 9, pp. 141–53. London: Hogarth Press and Institute of Psycho-Analysis, 1959. 3rd ed. 1964.

—. *Introductory Lectures on Psycho-Analysis. CPW 16.* 1963. 2nd ed. 1964.

Frisch, Max. *Andorra*. New York: Hill & Wang, 1964.

Gendlin, Eugene. *Focusing*. New York: Bantam, 1981.

Goldschmidt, H. L. *Freiheit für den Widerspruch*. Schaffhausen: Novalis, 1970.

Grimms' Tales for Young and Old: The Complete Stories. Translated by Ralph Mannheim. New York, London, Toronto, Sydney, Auckland: Doubleday, Anchor Books, 1983.

Hannah, Barbara. *Jung: His Life and Work; a Biographical Memoir*. Boston and London: Shambhala, 1991.

—. *Encounters with the Soul: Active Imagination as Developed by C. G. Jung*. Boston: Sigo Press, 1981.

Jacoby, Mario. *Psychotherapeuten sind auch Menschen: Übertragung und menschliche Beziehung in der Jungschen Praxis*. Olten: Walter, 1987.

Jacoby, Mario, Verena Kast and Ingrid Riedel. *Witches, Ogres, and the Devil's Daughter*. Boston and London: Shambhala, 1992.

Jung, Carl Gustav. *Collected Works (=CW)*. Edited by Gerhard Adler et al. Bollingen Series XX. Princeton: Princeton University Press, 1954 ff.

The Psychogenesis of Mental Disease. CW 3. 1960.

The Relations between the Ego and the Unconscious (1928). In *CW 7*. 2nd ed. 1970.

The Archetypes and the Collective Unconscious. CW 9/1. 2nd ed. 1968.

Mysterium Coniunctionis. CW 14. 2nd ed. 1970.

The Practice of Psychotherapy. CW 16. 2nd ed. 1966.

—. *Memories, Dreams, Reflections*. New York: Random House, Vintage, 1989.

—. *Letters 1: 1906-1950*. Edited by Gerhard Adler and Aniela Jaffé. Bollingen Series XCV: 1. Princeton: Princeton University Press, 1973.

Jung, Carl Gustav and Richard Wilhelm. *The Secret of the Golden Flower: A Chinese Book of Life*. San Diego: Harcourt Brace Jovanovich, 1970.

Kant, Immanuel. *Critique of Pure Reason*. New York: St. Martin's Press, 1965.

Kast, Verena. *Das Assoziationsexperiment in der therapeutischen Praxis*. 2nd ed. Fellbach: Bonz, 1988.

—. *The Creative Leap: Psychological Transformation through Crisis*. Wilmette (Illinois): Chiron Publications, 1990.

—. *Familienkonflikte im Märchen*. 3rd ed. Olten: Walter, 1986.

—. *Märchen als Therapie*. Olten: Walter, 1986.

—. *The Nature of Loving: Patterns of Human Relationship*. Wilmette: Chiron Publications, 1986.

—. *Sisyphos: The Old Stone--A New Way. A Jungian Approach to Midlife Crisis*. Einsiedeln (Switzerland): Daimon, 1991.

—. *Der Teufel mit den drei goldenen Haaren*. 7th ed. Stuttgart: Kreuz, 1987.

—. *A Time to Mourn: Growing through the Grief Process*.

Einsiedeln: Daimon, 1989.

—. *Traumbild Wüste: Von Grenzerfahrungen unseres Lebens*. Olten: Walter, 1986.

Katz, David. *Gestalt Psychology: Its Nature and Significance*. New York: Ronald Press, 1950. Reprint 1979.

Kurdische Märchen. Märchen der Weltliteratur. Düsseldorf and Cologne: Diederichs, 1978.

Lazarus, Arnold. *In the Mind's Eye: The Power of Imagery for Personal Enrichment*. New York: Guilford Press, 1984.

Lazarus, Arnold and Allen Fay. *I Can if I Want to*. New York: Warner, 1988.

Leuner, Hanscarl, ed. *Katathymes Bilderleben: Ergebnisse in Theorie und Praxis*. Berne, Stuttgart, Vienna: Huber, 1980.

—. *Lehrbuch des Katathymen Bilderlebens*. Berne: Huber, 1985.

Maass, Hermann. *Der Seelenwolf: Das Böse wandelt sich in positive Kraft*. Olten: Walter, 1984.

Mainberger, Gonsalv K. "Imagination." In *Die Psychologie des 20. Jahrhunderts*, vol. XIV, edited by G. Condrau. Zurich: Kindler, 1979.

Márquez, Gabriel Garcia. *Love in the Time of Cholera*. New York: Viking Penguin, 1989.

Moreno, M. "Der Traum: Imaginative Aktivität versus Interpretation." In *Analytische Psychologie. Zeitschrift für analytische Psychologie und ihre Grenzgebiete*, vol. 11, no. 2, 1980.
Müller, R. "Die aktive Imagination bei C. G. Jung." In

Analytische Psychologie, vol. 15, no. 3, 1984.

Neumann, Erich. *The Great Mother: An Analysis of the Archetype.* Bollingen Series XLVII. Princeton: Princeton University Press, 1963.

Norwegische Volksmärchen. Ed K. Strebe and T. Christianse. Düsseldorf and Cologne: Diederichs, 1967.

Overbeck, Gerd. *Krankheit als Anpassung: Der sozio-psychosomatische Zirkel.* Frankfurt/M.: Suhrkamp, 1984.

Petzold, Ernst and Achim Reindell. *Klinische Psychosomatik.* Heidelberg: Quelle und Meyer, 1980.

Phillipson, H. *A Short Introduction to the Object Relations Technique.* Windsor: NFER, 1973.

Pouplier, Mechthild. *Traumbild Fisch: Vom Leben in der Tiefe unserer Seele.* Olten: Walter, 1986.

Popper, Karl and John Eccles. *The Self and Its Brain: An Argument for Interactionism.* New York: Routledge, 1984.

Revers, Wilhelm Josef. *Der thematische Apperzeptionstest (TAT).* Berne: Huber, 1973.

Riess, Gisela. *Traumbild Feuer.* Olten: Walter, 1986.

Russische Volksmärchen. Ed. and tr. Xaver Schaffgotsch. Munich: Ellermann, n.d.

Sandler, J. "Gegenübertragung und Rollenübernahme." In *Psyche 4*, 1976.

Segal, Sydney and Michael Glicksman. "Relaxation and the

Perky Effect: The Influence of Body Position on Judgments of Imagery." *The American Journal of Psychology*, 1967, vol. 80, no. 2, pp. 257–62.

Sellberg, A. "Persönliche Erfahrungen mit dem Katathymen Bilderleben." In Hanscarl Leuner, ed. *Katathymes Bilderleben: Ergebnisse in Theorie und Praxis*. Berne, Stuttgart, Vienna: 1980.

Schultz, K. David. "Imagery and the Control of Depression." In Jerome L. Singer and Kenneth S. Pope, eds. *The Power of Human Imagination*. New York and London: Plenum, 1978.

Singer, Jerome L. *Imagery and Daydream: Methods in Psychotherapy and Behavior Modification*. New York: Academic, 1974.

Singer, Jerome L. and Kenneth S. Pope, eds. *The Power of Human Imagination*. New York and London: Plenum, 1978.

Shorr, Joseph E. *Psycho-Imagination Therapy*. New York: Intercontinental Medial Book Corp., 1972.

Starker, S. "Daydreaming Styles and Nocturnal Dreaming." In *Journal of Abnormal Psychology*, vol. 83, no. 1, 1974.

Strobel, H. "Aktive Imagination als Krisenintervention." In M. Pflüger, ed. *Kurzpsychotherapie und Krisenintervention in Sozialarbeit, Seelsorge und Therapie*. Fellbach, P.M., 1978.

—. "Methodik der Aktiven Imagination." In Ursula Eschenbach, ed. *Die Behandlung in der Analytischen Psycholgie II: Behandlung als menschliche Begegnung*. Fellbach: Bonz, 1981.

Studt, Hans H., ed. *Psychosomatik in Forschung und Praxis*. Munich, Vienna, Baltimore: Urban und Schwarzenberg, 1983.
Studt, Hans H., R. Frank, and D. Vaitl. "Alexithymie: Differentialdiagnostische Analyse aus verhaltenstheoretischer

Sicht." In Hans H. Studt, ed. *Psychosomatik in Forschung und Praxis*. Munich, Vienna, Baltimore: Urban und Schwarzenberg, 1983.

Van Egeren, L. F., B. W. Feather, and P. L. Hein. "Desensitization of Phobias: Some Psychophysiology Propositions." In *Psychopysiology*, 1971, vol. 8.

Von Franz, Marie-Louise. "Die aktive Imagination bei C. G. Jung." In Bitter, "Meditation in Religion und Psychotherapie." Stuttgart: Klett, 1958.

—. "Aktive Imagination in der Psychologie C. G. Jungs." In Bitter, *Praxis dynamischer Gruppenarbeit*. Stuttgart: Arzt und Seelsorger, 1972.

—. *C. G. Jung: Sein Mythos in unserer Zeit*. Stuttgart: Frauenfeld, 1972.

—. "The Process of Individuation." In *Man and His Symbols*, conceived and edited by Carl Gustav Jung. New York, London, Sidney, Auckland: Doubleday, Anchor Books, 1984, pp. 158–229.

Von Uexküll, Theodor and Wolfgang Wesiack. "Wissenschaftstheorie und psychosomatische Medizin: Ein bio-psychosoziales Modell." In Theodor von Uexküll, *Psychosomatische Medizin*. Ed. Rolf Adler et al. Munich, Vienna, Baltimore: Urban und Schwarzenberg, 1986.

Ware, R. C. "Handhabung der Übertragung/Gegenübertragung bei Frühgestörten als interpersonelle Form von aktiver Imagination." In *Analytische Psychologie. Zeitschrift für Analytische Psychologie und ihre Grenzgebiete*, vol. 11, no. 2, 1980.

Wilhelm, Richard and Carl Gustav Jung. *The Secret of the Golden*

Flower: A Chinese Book of Life. San Diego: Harcourt Brace Jovanovich, 1970.

Wilke, E. "Diagnostische und theoretische Aspekte der Arbeit mit dem Katathymen Bilderleben bei Patienten mit Colitis Ulcerosa und Morbus Crohn." In Hans H. Studt, ed. *Psychosomatik in Forschung und Praxis*. Munich, Vienna, Baltimore: Urban und Schwarzenberg, 1983.

Zigeunermärchen. Märchen der Weltliteratur. Cologne: Diederichs, 1962.